User-Centered Agile Methods

User-Centered Agile Methods

Hugh Beyer

ISBN: 978-3-031-01065-1   paperback
ISBN: 978-3-031-02193-0   ebook

DOI 10.1007/978-3-031-02193-0

A Publication in the Springer series
SYNTHESIS LECTURES ON HUMAN-CENTERED INFORMATICS

Lecture #10
Series Editor: John M. Carroll, *Penn State University*
Series ISSN
Synthesis Lectures on Human-Centered Informatics
Print 1946-7680   Electronic 1946-7699

Synthesis Lectures on Human-Centered Informatics

Editor
John M. Carroll, *Penn State University*

Human-Centered Informatics (HCI) is the intersection of the cultural, the social, the cognitive, and the aesthetic with computing and information technology. It encompasses a huge range of issues, theories, technologies, designs, tools, environments and human experiences in knowledge work, recreation and leisure activity, teaching and learning, and the potpourri of everyday life. The series will publish state-of-the-art syntheses, case studies, and tutorials in key areas. It will share the focus of leading international conferences in HCI.

User-Centered Agile Methods
Hugh Beyer
2010

Experience-Centered Design: Designers, Users, and Communities in Dialogue
Peter Wright and John McCarthy
2010

Experience Design: Technology for All the Right Reasons
Marc Hassenzahl
2010

Designing and Evaluating Usable Technology in Industrial Research: Three Case Studies
Clare-Marie Karat and John Karat
2010

Interacting with Information

Ann Blandford and Simon Attfield
2010

Designing for User Engagement: Aesthetic and Attractive User Interfaces
Alistair Sutcliffe
2009

Context-Aware Mobile Computing: Affordances of Space, Social Awareness, and Social Influence
Geri Gay
2009

Studies of Work and the Workplace in HCI: Concepts and Techniques
Graham Button and Wes Sharrock
2009

Semiotic Engineering Methods for Scientific Research in HCI
Clarisse Sieckenius de Souza and Carla Faria Leitão
2009

Common Ground in Electronically Mediated Conversation
Andrew Monk
2008

User-Centered Agile Methods

Hugh Beyer
InContext Design
www.InContextDesign.com

SYNTHESIS LECTURES ON HUMAN-CENTERED INFORMATICS #10

ABSTRACT

With the introduction and popularization of Agile methods of software development, existing relationships and working agreements between user experience groups and developers are being disrupted. Agile methods introduce new concepts: the Product Owner, the Customer (but not the user), short iterations, User Stories. Where do UX professionals fit in this new world? Agile methods also bring a new mindset—no big design, no specifications, minimal planning—which conflict with the needs of UX design.

This lecture discusses the key elements of Agile for the UX community and describes strategies UX people can use to contribute effectively in an Agile team, overcome key weaknesses in Agile methods as typically implemented, and produce a more robust process and more successful designs. We present a process combining the best practices of Contextual Design, a leading approach to user-centered design, with those of Agile development.

KEYWORDS

agile, agile development, scrum, xp, extreme programming, usability, usability engineering, HCI, UX, user experience, user-centered design, customer-centered design, human-centered design, iterative design, design, design methods, methodology, user interface design, user research, project management, user experience project management, human factors, prototyping, contextual inquiry, contextual design, user data collection, interactive design

To Karen Holtzblatt, a great collaborator

Contents

Bibliography

Author's Biography

CHAPTER 1

Introduction

Agile methods have transformed how developers think about organizing the development of a project. Rather than months (or years) of development, followed by months of field test leading up to a release, agile methods organize development into short iterations with continuous testing and a flexible release date. The agile approach promises to produce more useful and more reliable software, more quickly, and with better control than traditional development. Incorporating strong, user-centered techniques in agile development can only make the project stronger. But the origins and perspectives of agile methods are different from those of user-centered design, and this leads to confusion. It is the objective of this monograph to show how the two can be brought together into a powerful project development approach.

Several different approaches to agile development are currently popular: XP, Scrum, Feature Driven Development (FDD), and Crystal are a few. All these agile methods share core elements: short, well-defined iterations that deliver real user value; tight team processes for efficient development; minimal documentation of specifications; and continual feedback from stakeholders to validate progress. Agile methods also introduce a new development culture—values and attitudes that agile teams are expected to adopt. These include doing design up front is bad, internal documentation is bad, while face-to-face communication and collaboration are good.

To operate successfully in this new environment, the people doing user research, user interface design, and usability work need to understand the agile culture. Much of this culture can be helpful and supportive of working with end-users and incorporating user interface design into the development process. But there are elements of the culture, especially as it tends to be adopted by new teams, that make designing the user experience more difficult.

Most teams are still new to agile development, so no one is sure exactly how to behave. No one knows when an agile value should be treated like a rigid rule and when it should be taken as a guideline to be balanced against other concerns. When adopting agile methods, some teams take the process to extremes; others, more cautious, adopt only a few elements of agile development and see few benefits as a result.

In this monograph, we discuss the relationship between user-centered design and agile development, and we provide guidance through the competing claims and attitudes. We start with some description of agile processes as they now exist. In these sections, we cover the theoretical definitions of the approach provided by experts but also discuss the way we have seen processes and attitudes adopted in the real world, both in new and more experienced teams. Agile processes have not been adopted exactly the same way everywhere; we try to give readers a sense of how agile might look in the teams they encounter. Readers new to agile development will find an orientation here to the agile approach and should get some insight into how agile can both hinder and invite more in-depth involvement from the people designing the user experience.

We then provide a framework for understanding how agile development fits into the overall structure of a project, from deciding what to build through delivery. We provide an overview of Contextual Design (CD), a user-centered design process co-developed by the author which supports this range of activities, and show how user-centered design integrates with agile development. We end with some examples of different project structures.

A word on terminology: Throughout this monograph, we use "UX" (user experience) to refer to those roles involved in understanding users and designing the right system to support them. Activities of the UX team include user research and analysis, high-level design of the system as experienced by the users, specification of system behavior, high-level interaction design and screen layout, and testing proposed or completed designs with users (prototyping and usability test).

We refer to the user-visible design of the system itself as the user interface (UI). This is a general term covering both behavior and look. We use "visual design" for the design of the appearance of the product—detailed layout, color, and graphics. The skills required for visual design overlap those needed for UX design but are not identical—some very good UX professionals do not have the graphic design skills to create a good-looking UI, and some good visual designers know all about graphic design and layout but do not interact with users directly.

We will be careful of our use of the terms "user," "customer," and "stakeholder." UX professionals are used to making distinctions between these roles, but they are often blurred in the agile community. We prefer to reserve *user* or *end-user* for the person who interacts directly with the product or system to produce a desired result. *Indirect users* depend on the results of the system even if they do not use it directly.

Customers are the people who derive value from the system: users' management, the purchaser, possibly the IT department that has to maintain the system, and anyone else who has a say in adopting the system. (Watch out. The agile community sometimes uses "customer" to mean "user"—but this is an important distinction to maintain.)

Stakeholders are people in the development organization who depend on the system being correct. Management of the development team, the product owner, and the marketing team are all potential stakeholders.

Finally, we are not making a clear distinction about the type of product being created, whether it is an internal business system, a web site, a software product for sale, or a consumer product. Most of the issues and most of the processes are the same regardless of what is being created, and both agile development and user-centered design have been used for all types of product. Where it is necessary to make a distinction, we call out the difference explicitly.

CHAPTER 2

Common Agile Methods

Though agile development is a new movement in the industry, iterative development has a long and successful history. Agile enthusiasts point to the development of the space shuttle avionics in the 1970's, developed iteratively because of the "high risk" involved[1]. The initial development of WordPerfect in the 1980's was a classic agile project, as people in the company described it to us: Alan Ashton and Bruce Bastian developed the word processor for the city of Orem, Utah. They could sit with their users to discover problems, code fixes and enhancements in the afternoon, and give the secretaries a new version to try the next day. And Boehm described a "spiral model" of development in 1988[2].

Agile methods are popular now because they solve problems both for developers and for management. Developers created the methods because they felt powerless and out of control. Schedules, they felt, were dictated to them, requirements and project scope were changed throughout the project, and often, when the project shipped, users rejected it. Breaking the project into short sprints, freezing requirements during the sprint, and getting feedback throughout each sprint are ways of controlling the chaos of software development experienced by engineers

At the same time, management likes agile development because it gives them insight and control of a software project. Instead of waiting for months or years, only to discover that the final product is still months or years away, management gets a readout every few weeks. Management can always know exactly what is being worked on in a sprint and when that sprint will be done. Any problems come to light quickly.

The two most common agile methods in practice, at least in the United States, are Scrum and XP. We will briefly describe these two methods to provide background to the following discussion.

2.1 SCRUM

Scrum as defined to support product development dates back to 1986 but was described as a software development process by Schwaber and Beedle [3]. Scrum retains its roots as a product development framework, focusing more on project management and less on the specifics of coding procedures.

There is a lot of institutional support for Scrum—people can get trained and certified as "ScrumMasters," and it is easy to find Scrum coaches and Scrum training. As a project management framework, it is easy to understand and adopt. All this has made the approach quite popular.

Key elements of Scrum:

The product owner. The customer representative on a Scrum team is referred to as the product owner. Often played by the product manager or a marketing person, the product owner is the one person who defines what the project stakeholders need. It is up to the product owner to find out what the stakeholders and the end-users actually need, reconcile requirements, and communicate them to the team in a useful way. It is also up to the product owner to protect the team from churn caused by stakeholders changing their minds. This is allowed, but new requirements can only be thrown at the team at the beginning of a sprint.

Scrum explicitly defines the product owner as the single person who needs to be satisfied. If the deliverable is not successful but matches what the product owner asked for, the failure is solely that person's fault. This is a way of protecting the team from conflicting requirements imposed by different groups.

The team. All members of a Scrum team are equally committed and responsible for producing results. When describing commitment to the team, Scrum practitioners tell a story about a pig and a chicken who considered starting a restaurant. "We could serve ham and eggs," said the chicken. "I don't think that would work," said the pig. "I'd be committed, but you'd only be involved."

In the same way, Scrum team members are expected to be fully committed to the team—their success is tied to the team's success. Only these team members get a say in team decisions. Others, who are interested in the team's results but who are not themselves on the line, are considered "chickens"—they get to express an opinion but not make the decision.

The team is guided by a key individual, the *ScrumMaster*. This is the one who manages the process, runs the daily stand-up meeting, and runs the planning meetings to determine the product backlog and sprint backlog. The ScrumMaster may be a new role in the organization or may be played by the project manager—but not if the project manager is playing the product owner role. One person cannot play both roles.

The sprint. Development in Scrum is organized into *sprints*. Sprints are usually a month long, though some teams use shorter sprints. There is a cultural value in the agile community in favor of shorter sprints. This value is stronger in XP than in Scrum, but there is enough cross-fertilization that it affects Scrum teams as well.

A sprint starts by choosing *user stories* to implement in that sprint, choosing only as many stories as can be completed by the end of the sprint. Stories are chosen, tasks are defined to implement those stories, and team works starts. Stories and tasks are usually tracked using sticky notes on a wall so that they are visible to the entire team. They may be tracked online as well or only online, especially if the team is distributed.

Scrum defines several project management tools to track progress during a sprint, for example, (burn-down charts) which are maintained by the ScrumMaster and posted in prominent places. Each day starts with a stand-up meeting of the whole team to share progress and plan activities of the day. Participants stand, rather than sit, to encourage a short, focused meeting. A common format is for each team member to report on what they have done, what they plan to do this day, and what is getting in their way.

At the end of the sprint, there is a review of the work done in that sprint with the product owner and stakeholders. This is a short walkthrough—no more than four hours. In theory, at this point, the team's direction is re-evaluated, stories are reprioritized, and new stories may be written to respond to the feedback. In practice, many teams focus more on implementing the stories from the backlog than on rethinking project direction—and management often reinforces this more traditional mind-set.

At the end of the sprint, the team also reflects on its own processes, identifies problems, and discusses changes to make their process for the next sprint.

The backlog. Scrum projects start with product and sprint backlogs. Each backlog item is a unit of work to be completed within a sprint. User stories are the primary backlog items. At the beginning of the project, the team develops and prioritizes the product backlog; at the beginning of each sprint, the team chooses the items to implement for the sprint backlog.

Scrum does not define how the product owner knows what user stories to put on the backlog. The overall design or structure of the system is not represented explicitly, and agile practitioners generally do not value such a representation. There is usually no attempt to tie user stories together to show how a whole task or work process might be supported (though some teams do use large stories called "epics," which then need to be broken down into manageable chunks). Instead, the product owner is expected to capture individual system requirements as stories; the design will emerge from the code through iterative development. In practice, the backlog items are often derived from a Product Requirements Document (PRD) written by the product owner using traditional methods.

User stories. Each element of the desired solution is described in a *user story.* The story is written on an index card or sticky note. (Paper cards are used in theory; however, in practice, many teams use spreadsheets or special-purpose tools.) The story is not intended to be a full description of the feature—rather, it captures enough about the feature to remind everyone what the feature is. It is assumed that when a coder starts work on the feature, their first step will be to talk to the product owner and find out what to do, including what exact UI to implement, if the story requires a UI.

User stories must be small enough to be implemented within a single sprint, which means the product owner has to consult with developers to ensure they are not too large. Large, complex stories must be broken down into smaller stories, ideally, in such a way that each smaller story still makes sense when it is implemented on its own. User stories usually capture a single feature, though a single story may collect a few closely-related features.

One common format for writing stories is to write them in the form "As a [user role], I want [a feature] so that I can [achieve some goal]."

Example 2.1 Sample user stories.

As a network manager, I want a single view of the whole network so that I can identify and manage network problems.

As a salesperson, I want to capture customer information quickly so I can keep a history of my interactions with this customer.

2.2 XP

Much of the basis of XP came out of work at Chrysler Comprehensive Compensation. This was an internal project where both users and developers were both part of the same company. Reflecting this history, XP tends to assume that end-users really are local and really can be on the team. XP also tends to assume that delivering frequent updates to customers is not a problem: that building and shipping a release is quick and easy, and that rolling out an implementation to all customers is easy. *Extreme Programming Explained* [4] is a good, readable introduction to XP.

The elements of XP most relevant to our discussion are the following:

The customer. XP assumes that a real, experienced, end-user can be a full team member. They refer to this person as the "customer," somewhat confusingly for UX practitioners. The XP customer is empowered to decide what is or is not useful in the product. At the high level, they determine the priority of features and set the order of implementation (working with developers to make sure the order makes sense technically). At the low level, working with developers and UX designers, they define the detailed system design, look, layout, and interaction to meet their needs.

In practice, XP teams recognize that real, dedicated end-users are hard to come by as team members. Most teams also recognize that end-users are not designers and cannot necessarily make good UI decisions. So, on most XP teams, the customer is a role played by one person or a team of several internal people, usually including the product owner or project manager, business analysts if any, and key stakeholders on the business side if an IT system is being developed[5]. UX professionals are usually included on the customer team as well.

The result is that the customer role on an XP team is usually played by neither user, customer, nor stakeholder, as we have defined them. Yet they are tasked with representing all three perspectives to the team and reconciling them where they conflict.

The release planning game. It is typical of XP to call release planning a game: XP values highly interactive and highly interpersonal interactions over formal documents and structured interactions. In the release planning game, the XP customer arrives with user story cards describing everything that they think is needed in the next release of the product. Developers then estimate the implementation time required for each story.

The result of the release planning game is a rough estimate of when the project will be completed, based on the total implementation time of the selected stories and team's measured capacity. XP emphasizes tracking how much work a team can do in a sprint (the team's *velocity*) and using the measure to limit the work they commit to. Stories can be added or removed from the release to change the delivery date.

Iterations. In XP, sprints are referred to as *iterations*. Each iteration starts with iteration planning and ends with customer acceptance (both described below). There is a strong cultural prejudice in the XP community towards shorter iterations. Two weeks is typical, and working in one-week iterations gives a team bragging rights. XP provides few tools for tracking progress during an iteration—iterations are too short to need much project management.

Every user story accepted for implementation during an iteration must be entirely completed within that iteration, including passing all unit and customer acceptance tests. There is a strong cultural value against counting any progress towards implementing a story if it is not completely done and passing all tests. In practice though, many teams do not entirely live up to this value. Exactly what is considered "done done" tends to be an ongoing debate.

Iteration planning. Each iteration starts with an iteration planning session. This is a face-to-face meeting in which the team selects the stories to be implemented during an iteration. The XP customer chooses the stories most important to provide value. In theory, every iteration provides real customer value, so that as soon as the first iteration is complete, the team already has a system that the customer could pick up and use. In fact, it takes more than one or two weeks to make a useful product, so teams focus on producing a baselevel that builds and runs correctly.

The team uses their velocity to decide how many stories to select. If they can implement 40 points in an iteration, once they have selected stories adding up to 40 points, no more work can be planned into that iteration. Once stories are selected, the developers break down the stories into tasks that can be done by different people on the team.

Any rework has to be done during iterations. Rework includes bug fixes and functionality changes, for example, if an implemented feature turns out to be unacceptable to users. There are several ways to handle rework. Some teams treat it as overhead: they reserve something like 20% of their story points, planning to spend that time on rework and bug fixes. Other teams (and this is the author's preference) plan rework using story cards. Every item of rework gets its own card and its own time estimate. The XP customer is responsible for prioritizing rework against implementing new stories.

Because rework and new user stories can be introduced at any point, in response to user feedback, some new XP teams go overboard. They tell management that they cannot say what they will build or when it will be completed because everything is iterative now[6]. A business needs predictability, so this phase is usually not allowed to last long, but it does create difficulties in trying to work with such a team while it lasts.

In practice, many teams have difficulty scheduling rework at all. Feeling pressure to get as much functionality done as fast as possible, they do not feel they can reserve time for rework or move existing stories out to do rework. The team is focused on getting stories off the backlog list. Revisiting "done" stories slows that down. When this happens, there is really only one shot at getting a story right—once it is implemented, changing it is hard.

Acceptance testing. XP culture is strongly test-driven, and it values automated testing highly. Teams are expected to do nightly builds and run their entire suite of unit tests nightly; test-driven design, in which the tests are written first, is an approved practice.

These attitudes spill over to customer acceptance testing. Teams want customer acceptance tests to be automatable and, ideally, defined along with the user stories. These automated acceptance tests can show whether the implementation meets the technical requirements defined by the user story. Actual acceptability—

whether the system is useful to and usable by end-users—is not addressed by XP except through the involvement of the XP customer. But XP teams generally recognize that it is important to know whether the implementation meets the needs of actual users. Quality Assurance groups test the whole product at the end of each iteration, often as team members. Usability testing may also be performed at the end of an iteration or afterwards.

Development practices. XP defines a number of development practices intended to support rapid development with little documentation. Pair programming, test-driven development, collective code ownership, and the nightly build are a few of these. Though these are important, they have little impact on how UX people fit into an agile team, and we will not discuss them here.

Because Scrum and XP address slightly different problems, they dovetail with each other fairly easily. Scrum provides the overall project management; XP provides more detailed guidance on running development. This is how many teams use them together.

However, XP practices are difficult and disruptive to the daily lives of developers. They may be valuable, but they require discipline to implement. Scrum, on the other hand, structures project management but makes fewer demands on developers. Therefore, when teams are new to agile development, they often adopt the backlog and sprints from Scrum but do not really change their development practices. UX professionals need to recognize how far along a development team has progressed in agile adoption in order to understand the best way to integrate with that team.

CHAPTER 3

Agile Culture

When agile methods are brought into an organization, they create confusion and uncertainty, as does any organizational change. This is a natural part of the learning process of incorporating, adapting, and institutionalizing a new way of working. To be successful, UX professionals need to learn the language and attitudes of agile development. The new values and culture will make some established ways of working more difficult, but properly understood, they also open up opportunities for better integrating UX into the development process.

The following agile cultural values have the potential to interfere with the working relationship between UX professionals and software developers. By understanding the value and its intent, UX professionals can leverage the value to promote user-centered development within an agile team.

3.1 THERE IS ONLY ONE TEAM

The whole team is responsible for the whole team's work. No one can deny responsibility. If one part of the project has a problem, it is everybody's problem. The team needs to work tightly together, ideally, co-located in a single room. There should be no special skills or ownership; everyone on the team should be able to work on any part of the product. (This value is stronger on XP teams than on Scrum teams.)

But it is hard for a team to be as cohesive as agile methods envision. Often, a team must be distributed for practical or business reasons. Many team members, especially the UX experts, cannot be dedicated to a single team full-time, instead being spread across multiple projects. And there are special skills which take time to develop, and which tend to be concentrated in just one or a few team members—including, of course, the skill of UX design.

Since agile methods started as methods for developing code, teams are often uncertain how non-coders fit into the agile team. Sometimes, UX expertise is simply ignored, under the assumption that the team's product owner can provide all the user interface knowledge required. Sometimes UX professionals are explicitly assumed to be part of the customer team, supporting the product owner. It has been known for teams to go to the other extreme, treating UX professionals as full team members—but then, believing that all team members should be interchangeable, want them to learn to code, and want coders to design UIs.

The UX leverage point. UX professionals can use this "one team" expectation to their advantage. They should be recognized as full team members, albeit part-time if necessary—they should participate as pigs (committed) not chickens (involved). As team members, UX people need to educate the team on what UX is all about and what is needed to design a reasonable user interface. If there is no time to complete a UI design task, shared ownership suggests this is a problem for the whole team, not only that of the UX designer. Conversely, simple UIs may need to be designed by other team members with the UX designer's guidance, leaving the UX designer to focus on those central or complex UIs where their expertise makes the most difference.

3.2 THE USER IS ON THE TEAM

The user or user representative is assumed to be a full member of the team. Scrum makes this the responsibility of the product owner. Other teams define a customer team, which may include more than one person. The customer team is responsible for representing the user, prioritizing work to ensure the team delivers real value, and making decisions about what will or will not work for the user—including helping to define low-level functionality and UI details.

Originally, agile methods simply assumed the real user could be on the team, and many agile teams are still unclear as to what that means. They do not appreciate the distinction between an end-user, a purchaser, and an internal stakeholder, and they do not understand why the distinction matters. Some teams even claim that for their purposes, the distinction does not matter: if they have met the requirements of the internal stakeholder or product owner, they have done their job, whether or not the end-user is happy.

Agile methods tend to overlook the real issues getting in the way of collecting valid end-user feedback. They tend to assume that users can say what they want if asked; that users can articulate their tasks, motives, and goals; and that users can devote extensive time to guiding developers—none of which are true. They tend to assume that if the team meets the requirements of stakeholders or purchasers, the system will work for end-users—not recognizing their different points of view. And they do not define how to handle development for a market when there is no dedicated user at all. Agile methods do not define how people playing the customer role on the team can learn what the real end-user needs and how they can accurately represent those needs to the developers.

The UX leverage point. The expertise of UX professionals is particularly valuable here. By now, most product teams have learned that they need help understanding their users and their users' needs. Adopting agile methods makes that understanding even more critical. The UX contribution can be to provide the methods and expertise for building detailed user knowledge so that a team can operate effectively even without a real end-user dedicated to the team.

3.3 PLANS AND ARCHITECTURAL WORK ARE A WASTE OF TIME

From the agile perspective, the world changes. Requirements change. Management goals change. Therefore, if you spend months working on a design, it is highly likely that most of that design will never be implemented as envisioned. It is better to do something small and get it done quickly, get feedback, and build on it with no overall plan, rather than spend a lot of time on a plan that will never be implemented.

Because agile methods assume that in a changing world up-front plans are a waste of time, they tend to denigrate any sort of up-front planning or design activity. It is not apparent to them that end-user work practice is quite stable—that how people do their jobs and the goals they must accomplish change very little over time. It is not apparent that fundamental requirements are stable in consequence. It has been the experience of developers that every time users are shown a system that implements the requirements the developers were given, the users ask for something different. This makes it *look* like the requirements have changed. It is not apparent that the users were unable to articulate their real needs in the first place.

Agile methods do not address ideation, deciding what problems the product is to solve, or designing an approach to solve them. Agile processes start with story cards, which define the basic behavior of the product; however, they do not define how those story cards are generated. Agile development methods do not define how to invent an integrated experience to support users' work with a cohesive system.

Most agile experts understand this while many developers new to agile do not. The result is a mismatch between the problem and the method: teams attempt to get the requirements right by sitting in a room with the product owner and writing story cards, without any explicit design of the whole system.

Agile methods have no specific techniques to support any part of designing the user interface: the organization, structure and layout of the user interface into windows, pages, or screens; the particular design of user interaction elements such as buttons, pulldown menus, direct manipulation and so forth; and the details of graphic design that defines the appearance of these elements.

So, "pure" agile methods have no way to develop a complete understanding of users and their needs; no way to invent and structure a coherent solution; and no way to design a consistent user experience, interaction paradigm, and appearance across the product.

While experts understand this, new and enthusiastic agile teams tend to assume all the methods that apply to writing code will apply just as well to UI design. So they suggest solutions drawn from agile development: Why not pair a coder with a UI designer to develop screens together? Why not design an entire screen in the same one-week iteration as the code is written? Why not implement the UI first and test it with end-users afterwards?

The UX leverage point. This is another problem solved by UX techniques. There is a growing recognition in the agile community[7;8] that much of the ideation work should happen before the development work gets started. Sometimes called a Phase 0, sometimes treated as a requirements definition phase that precedes development, this is when UX designers should contribute by understanding users, representing user work practice and tasks, and designing the appropriate information architecture, function and high-level structure to meet users' needs. The goal at this point is to design and validate the core of the proposed system so that user stories can be written with confidence that these stories define a successful product.

It is also possible for the UX team to run a parallel stream to the iterative development process. This frees research and design tasks from the strict timebox of individual sprints, allowing the UX team to maintain design coherence while still participating in the work of the sprints.

3.4 FACE-TO-FACE COMMUNICATION IS BETTER THAN DOCUMENTATION

In a changing world, thorough documentation takes too long to write, is obsolete as soon as written, and does not communicate well anyway. It is difficult and cumbersome to write in human language a complete description of how a function is to behave. Once written, it provides no value to the customer. It still has to be translated into code. And there is no way to show that the description is correct or useful.

The agile value says it is better to have the people who know what is needed (the user) talk directly to the people building the product (the developer) during development. That way, all the nuances of the function can be discussed and agreed upon. It is better to define the function once, in code, and have the user immediately verify that the implemented behavior is what they intended.

But, as discussed above, the user usually cannot be on the team and cannot devote the time to detailed discussions of every system function, so daily face-to-face interaction is often impossible. Furthermore, even if it were possible, users cannot reliably articulate their needs or provide feedback on unfamiliar design ideas.

The UX leverage point. The UX team member has the skills to understand users' needs in depth and to translate those needs into specific system behavior. This suggests a close working relationship between the UX designer and the developers on the team. It should be the norm to have daily discussions with one developer or another on how to implement the UI for a story. In addition, UX professionals may also need to let go of some of their own documentation, relying more on sketches and discussions and less on fully-rendered UI designs.

3.5 SHORT SPRINTS ARE GOOD. SHORTER SPRINTS ARE BETTER

The work of an agile team is structured sprints. Each sprint ends with building a complete version of the product. In theory, this baselevel could actually be delivered to users, tested by the users, and their feedback used to reprioritize the work of the next sprint.

Agile methods assume useful work can be started and completed within a single sprint, and agile teams tend to believe that shorter sprints are better than longer ones. At the same time, agile methods dictate that each sprint should deliver real customer value.

Taken too literally, this is, of course, impossible. For most interesting projects, a single two-or four-week sprint cannot deliver useful value. It will take many such sprints before a product has accumulated enough features to be of practical use.

So most teams compromise. Perhaps, the initial sprints can, at least, be installed and run at customer sites even if they are not useful. Early sprints may deliver a reasonable user interface with severe limitations of function or some useful function with a bare-bones user interface. The function may work in the simplest case, but not yet deal with all the real situations that will be required of the final product.

Where needed function takes longer than a sprint to implement, it is broken into multiple stories. Each story by itself must work technically, but it might not be useful to real people. UX work may need to be broken up in the same way and may need to be separated from the implementation work for the same function so that the UX work can be done an iteration ahead.

Though we have discussed the compromises teams make to deal with problems of real projects, it is useful to keep the underlying reason for the short sprints in mind: It should be possible, at the end of any sprint, to decide the project is over and that the work done to date will ship. A project should work towards achieving shippable code in as few sprints as possible, to give themselves flexibility in the rest of the project. And even from the first sprint, all function that is present should work. The code should be production quality and bug-free—no putting off bug fixing to the end of the project.

The name for this is *technical debt:* work that has been put off but that must be done eventually before the product can ship. Another sort of technical debt is architectural work, such as code refactoring (restructuring the function and interface of several modules to simplify their interaction). The code may work correctly now, but if it is getting more and more complex, it will become impossible to continue to extend it. Sooner or later, the technical debt must be repaid by taking time to do the refactoring work.

The UX leverage point. UX professionals should insist the team apply these same standards to the UI. At the end of a sprint, the UI should be UI-bug free. All user interfaces should be operational, acceptably usable, conformant with standards, and representing the company's brand. Failure to maintain the UI at this level in each iteration is as unacceptable as failing to maintain the code at this level because it equally prevents the product from being shippable.

With this perspective, the entire team has a stake in ensuring that the UX work is done as part of the sprint. If there is not enough time to do user interviews and prototypes in the same sprint as the implementation, it is acceptable to break the UX work into a separate story. This is just an extension of techniques agile teams already use to break down larger stories into manageable chunks.

Putting off usability testing or losing control of design coherence across the UI because the different parts are being iterated independently is just another form of debt—call it *design debt*. Just like technical debt, design debt will need to be paid eventually, or the quality of the product will suffer. To limit design debt, one of the ongoing UX activities must be to maintain an architectural view of the entire product and make sure that it stays consistent, coherent, and usable. This is the UX equivalent of code refactoring.

3.6 CONTINUAL FEEDBACK GUIDES THE PROJECT

One reason for short sprints is to start providing real value as soon as possible. The other is to get feedback on each sprint as it is developed. This feedback ensures that the project stays on track— that each sprint is getting closer to a useful product. Short sprints reduce the lag between the time a decision is taken and when that decision is tested and proven to be correct. Ideally, a two-week sprint means all decisions will be tested within two weeks at most. The team can never get more than two weeks off track.

Within a sprint, developers expect to work with the user (or representative) to decide exactly how to implement a story—how the feature is to behave, what the UI should look like, and what special cases must be accounted for. At the end of each sprint, the sprint, itself, is tested with stakeholders to ensure it meets their needs.

Unfortunately, it is rare that developers can meet with the end user throughout the sprint. Additionally, the feedback session at the end of a sprint is usually a "show and tell" or demo, a quick walkthrough of the product with comments and reactions collected and recorded. Such a review can do two things: it provides a sense of closure and celebration for the development team; and it can reveal basic miscommunications and glaring errors in the team's work. But it cannot ensure that the system actually works for its users. Stakeholders may sign off, but there is no guarantee that the project will be successful.

The UX leverage point. It is the UX team member who has the skills to get real user feedback into the iterative process. Real validation of the work requires that the team test the product with users in their own work context, working through examples of their own work tasks[9]. Developers, in general, do not have the skills or aptitude for this kind of work. UX people do, and they can do it on behalf of the team.

Within the sprint (or the sprint before implementation), UX designers define the precise user interface for a new feature either on behalf of the product owner or as part of the agile customer team. This low-level design can and should be tested with users before being implemented. Some developers feel this testing is unnecessary because with short sprints, a design can be coded and put in front of users very quickly. But we have already seen that actually revising a completed feature is hard for many teams; and for all teams, we should maintain the value of a minimal lag between design and validation. If UX designers can design, test, and iterate a screen design directly with users faster than it can be developed and iterated in code, this is just another way of reducing the lag.

3.7 HOWTHESE VALUES GO WRONG IN PRACTICE

The values driving agile development result in an effective approach to software development. Unfortunately, product development is more than just coding. Real-world organizations impose constraints that agile methods do not address. And new teams, lacking experience in agile development, are prone to compromise the very aspects of agile methods that matter most. (Chung and Drummond [10] offer some stories to illustrate how this happens.)

We often see development teams new to agile that have no real user presence on the team, and, indeed, that have no real user feedback of any sort. In a typical scenario, the product manager does his or her best to represent the user needs to the team, but the resources available to them are limited. They may contribute to writing user stories, but it is likely they wrote a Product Requirements Document (PRD) first because that's what they are used to. That PRD is produced using traditional methods—not including field research—and often represents the perspective of managers or buyers, rather than the detailed needs of end-users.

In the product planning meeting, the team writes user stories by reading through the PRD and pulling stories out of it. These stories may be prioritized with input from the product manager, but development teams have been prioritizing their own development for a very long time, and it is easy to fall back into those ways. The UX or Usability group, being busy, is often not involved at this stage.

Once the product planning meeting completes, that defines the product. Agile development may envision replanning at the end of each sprint, but everyone knows that management will hold the team responsible for implementing the user stories derived from the PRD.

The team then works in sprints, usually of a month each, pulling user stories off the backlog and implementing them. There is no real attempt to implement the unfamiliar and difficult coding disciplines that ensure quality (test-first design, pair programming, automated testing, and so on). The stand-up meeting that should start the day drags on too long, so it is abandoned. Bugs are tracked on a separate bug list, but fixing them is treated as a side activity, and they accumulate over time.

The UX team is usually spread far too thin; each UX designer is assigned to several product teams. They rush from team to team, trying to sketch reasonable designs for the team's user stories in the time they have. There's certainly no time for customer visits, prototyping, or information architecture.

At the end of each sprint, the team builds a baselevel and shows a demo to the product manager and other stakeholders. There is no attempt to check whether the baselevel delivers useful value to users, and there is no commitment to reworking stories anyway. There is no real attempt to reevaluate the user story backlog; the team just chooses the next set of stories to work on and starts on it.

Though many teams have implemented agile methods successfully, we see situations like the above scenario far too often. UX designers trying to fit in to such a team are adding additional complications to a process that is already broken. It is no surprise if the result is painful. We can do better.

CHAPTER 4

Best Practices for Integrating UX with Agile

Fundamentally, agile development comes down to this: develop in short iterations and test progress at each iteration with real user feedback. However, getting that real user feedback is not possible without the skills and techniques developed by the UX community. Integrating UX with agile development is not only possible, it is critical to the success of agile methods.

Already, we are seeing best practices emerge for such a combined process. These practices are being implemented in agile companies across the industry and provide a baseline for a workable development process. Many of these practices are identified in Martin, Biddle and Noble's survey[11] of agile teams across multiple companies. They reveal elements that must be included in a successful integrated approach. These best practices enable a team to address the potential weaknesses of agile development directly by:

- Providing space for understanding the user and envisioning a coherent solution;

- Collecting real, end-user feedback during sprints;

- Supporting real iteration—reworking the design in response to user feedback.

4.1 GET USER FEEDBACK FROM REAL USERS IN CONTEXT

For reasons we discuss below, the experience of the UX community shows there is no substitute for talking to the actual end-users of a proposed product or system directly, in their own workplace.

Originally, agile methods tended to finesse this need by specifying a customer or product owner role and leaving it undefined how the role was to function. This bias came from the history of some early agile projects. They were internal systems for internal users, and it was in fact not too difficult to walk over to a user, sit down beside them, and talk about how the system should be changed.

But, on most projects, it is no longer so easy. It is important to for the organization to recognize that there are real problems getting in the way of good user feedback and to recognize the limitations of the mechanisms that projects often use. UX people need to know how to talk to the organization about the need to augment existing methods with user research. The following points are familiar to UX professionals, but we have found they can be new to even quite senior agile developers. Goguen[12], Greenbaum and Kyng[13], and Wixon and Ramey[14] discuss these and other issues in collecting good user feedback in more depth.

Users are not good at articulating what they do. This is the problem of *tacit knowledge:* users have internalized the details of how they work. When asked questions about what they do, what problems they have, and what they need, the details of their own work are hard for them to recall. So the requirements they give are inaccurate and incomplete.

Users want to be helpful. Agile methods attempt to overcome the problem of tacit knowledge by delivering early and often. When users attempt to use the system to do their own work, they discover and report on problems.

But users tend to assume that to be helpful, they should respond to the system they were given. They may report on some minor inconvenience in that system; they are much less likely to explain that what they really need is another system entirely, or that the bulk of their work is spent on another task, or that what they are really doing is collecting and preparing all their data in a spreadsheet and then using the designed system just for data entry.

Users are not available as team members. Real users have real jobs. It is not reasonable to expect them to attend a daily meeting or to be interrupted every minute for questions about the details of a UI. Often, a business organization will insulate users from persistent developers by appointing user representatives to act as an interface. But the more they interface with developers, the less they do the real job. Some organizations establish business analysts, but generally, business analysts focus on defining business rules, processes, and data elements. They do not usually have interaction design skills. When making a product for a market, users are not even in the same company. And, of course, whether internal or external, users are often not located anywhere near the development team.

Surrogate users aren't. Product development organizations typically handle this problem either by putting surrogate users on the team or using marketing methods to find out more about them. There is real value in both methods, but by themselves, they are incomplete.

Surrogate users are never a good stand-in for real end-users. The managers of end-users describe how they wish the work was done, or how they think it ought to be done, not how it actually is done in their organizations. A new system may intentionally change and simplify the work practice, but if the team does not understand the real issues and real workarounds—which are often invisible to management—they cannot account for them in the new design.

Hiring users away from their organizations to be on the team full time has been tried but is also of limited value. Intentionally or not, they tend to take on the perspectives and values of the development team. "We found out our users representatives were being too nice to us," was one team's comment that tried this[15].

Product owners as defined by Scrum also do not make good user surrogates. They may be responsible for representing all the stakeholders of a system, including end-users, the customer who makes the purchase decision, and the internal stakeholders. But they are not any of these people and need mechanisms for understanding them and their needs just as much as any other project team member.

Marketing methods do not collect design data. Product development organizations attempt to use marketing methods such as surveys and focus groups to define products. But these methods provide high-level information about attitudes and desires. They do not reveal how users do work, define what system they need, or what such a system should do. Neither do they provide low-level detail about the requirements of system function and behavior such as how a task is structured, interactions within a work group, detailed steps users perform, how they collaborate in accomplishing a task, or the context and constraints on how the work is done. Marketing methods are good at collecting sales points and market requirements; they do not collect design data.

So, any effective user-centered agile process must include real user research: finding out who the end-users are and how they work; analyzing the tasks they do and the strategies they use to achieve those tasks; getting quick feedback on design ideas and on system baselevels to determine whether the project is on track; and testing designs against success criteria. The process must also support discovering the requirements of the users' management and purchasers and of internal business stakeholders.

Online data collection is incomplete. In this age of web-enabled apps, it is easy to instrument the apps themselves and use the data collected to guide development. Different versions of a design can be posted and usage data compared; click-throughs and pause times can be measured. Quick surveys can be popped up to collect data in the moment.

But although this kind of data may usefully augment field research, it is limited in the same way as more traditional market research methods. A survey can gather data on questions the designers thought to ask and that the user is aware enough of to respond to— but much of work practice is tacit. An instrumented app can report on what the users did but not why, or what they were trying to accomplish, or what the larger work task was. Any data collected this way will start from the assumption that it is the right app. The team will not discover that there are other opportunities they do not know about.

4.2 A PHASE 0 TO DEFINE SYSTEM SCOPE AND STRUCTURE

Much of the agile community, especially from the coding side, is driven by a strong skepticism of any sort of up-front planning. "Big Design Up Front" (BDUF), they call it. Also: YAGNI ("You Ain't Gonna Need It"), meaning that most of the big plans you have in your head will never turn out to be useful or relevant once you get to the point of implementing them. Business direction will change, user requirements will change, or the evolution of the design itself will make your idea irrelevant.

But successful projects that have significant user interfaces and have a significant impact on how users work have found that some level of up-front design is necessary[16]. (The Martin, Biddle, and Noble paper[11] refers to this as BPUF—Big Picture Up Front.)

Practically, projects discover the need for BPUF as soon as they sit down to write story cards. Suppose a team is developing an online newsreader. Think about the questions that must be answered before a story card can be written: What are the possible news sources? How should they be represented to the user? How should they be organized? Can the system organize them or must the user be able to, or both? What should the first screen contain? Should it show all new news items, or should it prioritize, and if so how? The questions are almost endless.

And each story card the team writes captures an element of a design that they never thought through, never represented in any concrete way, and which impacts the user's world in ways that are completely implicit and undesigned.

In theory, any problems will be resolved through iterations with the user. That is what agile is all about: keep iterating and fixing until the product works.

In fact, these problems cannot be entirely solved through iterations. As mentioned above, even in the best possible scenario, users will only renovate on what they are given. Unless a system is completely hopeless, they will not throw it out and tell the developers to start again with something different. So only about 20% of the overall system can be changed. The base assumptions and core structure are simply not amenable to stepwise change *within practical product timelines.* To counter a common argument heard in agile circles: it is true that evolution produced humans from single-cell proto-organisms using nothing but stepwise refinement. But evolution had millions of years to do it. Product teams do not.

And in the real world schedule limitations will be determinative. Any engineering project will only tolerate reworking the same design element so many times. Any product or business manager will only tolerate so much deviation from the initial project scope. Most agile projects struggle to get any rework time into their schedule at all. Once a user story is implemented, there is *no* time to go back and rework it in the project plan. The rework could be written into a new story and reprioritized at the next sprint planning meeting, but then some other committed story would go unimplemented. Unless the problem is a real show-stopper, that reprioritization is unlikely to happen.

Furthermore, iterating an existing solution will inevitably focus on fixing problems with that solution. What if the real opportunity is not in fixing problems with the current solution but recognizing that a different approach is needed? For example, the spreadsheet was invented when Dan Bricklin recognized that computer technology could be applied to the problem of manipulating accounting (paper) spreadsheets. Calculator technology existed at the time, but no amount of stepwise iteration would be likely to lead from number manipulation to an electronic spreadsheet.

If a team gets past writing user stories without any big-picture design, the next point where they will feel the lack of it is during sprints. In theory, a developer can go to the user and ask detailed questions about how a story should be implemented. In practice, this theoretical user is a product owner or a UX designer.

The programmer might ask: "What is more important to show: breaking news, or a story the user is actively following? What should be pushed to the top of the page?" If our user surrogate were honest, the answer would likely be, "Darned if I know." Unless they have worked with users in the field, how can they possibly answer such a detailed question correctly? The actual answer they give is usually something like, "Do it this way, that should work." This is a guess, dressed up in professional language. Without a solid understanding of the users to back it up, one of agile development's core drivers—immediate feedback—is broken.

Instead, problems with the design for a user story are not discovered until the story is implemented, built into an iteration, and shown to users. Even if the problem is discovered, and often it is not, a great deal of work has already gone into a wrong implementation. This rework is unnecessary.

Finally, but equally important in this day of sophisticated user interfaces, designing a coherent and consistent user experience across the whole product means that the entire UI must be designed together. If one part is changed, the impact of the changes on the whole system must be considered. This is very different from implementation design, so developers tend not to appreciate how important it is. When designing code, the goal is to separate each module from every other, so that each module of code can be modified and reimplemented without affecting any other module. Sometimes, this separation breaks down, and the relationship between modules has to be re-thought and several modules re-implemented together. This *code refactoring* is considered a major task, more difficult than ordinary coding.

For all these reasons, an effective agile process will make room for some high-level, up-front user research and high-level design, tested and iterated with users. This is often called a *phase 0,* or sprint 0. (We prefer the former name, as it better communicates the scope of the work.) User research grounds the agile customer team in the real user work practice, culture, goals, strategies, and issues. The high-level design sketches a systemic response to the user work practice, within the defined scope for the project, meeting the business needs of the organization. It also defines the groundwork for the user experience, defining consistent layout and interaction paradigms across the system.

This design, itself, even though high-level and provisional in its details, needs to be tested and iterated with customers. This realizes another core agile value discussed above: reduce the time lag between when a decision is made and when it is validated[4]. With a validated high-level design in hand, user stories can be written in confidence that they make sense and will deliver a system the user wants. We will discuss the structure of a phase 0 in Chapter 5, below.

4.3 UI DESIGN DONE ONE ITERATION AHEAD

It is hard for developers to appreciate how much work goes into a good UI design. Accordingly, processes designed by and for developers—as most agile processes are—often do not allow enough time for UX work to be done. Many agile proponents do not understand why it is hard to design the UI for a component, test it, do the graphic rendering, and communicate it to the developer, all within a few days, while still leaving enough time for the component to be coded, integrated, and tested within a two-week sprint.

Successful agile teams usually give the UX designers room to breathe by having them start on a component design one or more sprints ahead of coding. This way the UX team gets the whole of a sprint to do their UI design and user testing. The testing can and should be iterative with users—which means that the resulting design is refined with users, even if there is little time to rework stories in the development process.

Then in the following sprint, the UX team member can communicate the detailed UI to the developer, who gets the whole of that sprint to do the implementation. Meanwhile, the UX designers, in parallel, start on the UI design of stories for the iteration after that[17].

4.4 VALIDATION DONE ONE ITERATION BEHIND

Agile methods tend to be structured as though the last thing that has to happen is integration testing. Code a story, unit test it, integrate it into the code base, show it to the product owner, and it is done. Quality Assurance (QA) or User Acceptance Testing (UAT) is given a role in the process, but that role is limited by the short sprints. Generally, QA can do a reasonable job within the iterations by working closely and incrementally with developers as stories are checked in; generally, user acceptance testing cannot. A short presentation at the end of the sprint (as described, for example by Schwaber[18]) is *not* a realistic acceptance test.

Doing real user testing necessitates, first, bringing real users in or going out to them. It requires walking through the product with the user's own real-world examples. It requires that all the stories for the iteration be completed so that the interaction between new features can be investigated, It demands time to understand the implications of the users' feedback, which is always more complex than pass/fail. And it requires time to rework the parts of the system that have problems.

Realistically, it is very hard to do all this within an already-short sprint without making the iteration too short to do useful work. Even if such testing were possible, it does not require the whole team, and they need something to do while it is going on.

So, successful agile projects have found it effective to do their real testing with users one sprint behind the implementation. The sprint completes and the internal QA and UAT processes confirm that, to the best of the project team's ability to determine, they have correctly implemented the stories of that sprint. Then, during the following sprint, UX people can take that baselevel to customers, walk through real examples with it, and bring back problems and fixes to be addressed in the following sprint.

This practice also supports large-scale agile projects. In such efforts, the product of an agile team is, itself, just a component in a larger system. Time is needed to integrate the components from all the development teams and do integration testing. All this work can also be easily done one iteration behind[19].

4.5 PARALLEL UX STREAM

As mentioned above, ensuring the user experience of a product is coherent and consistent is a full-time job. Unlike refactoring, which is a special case, the UX team *always* needs to be concerned with overall consistency. Furthermore, there are usually larger constraints on the UI of the product. An individual agile team may be only implementing one part of a larger system. It may be implementing one product in a suite or one component of a product. The UI for their team part, must be coherent within itself and also within the larger product or suite. It must also conform with whatever standards or guidelines the company mandates.

So, the UX team needs to maintain a larger focus than just the product delivered by the team. They are always looking at both the design of individual screens and at the larger system they are a part of. Maintaining this wider focus is very hard in the time-compressed world of agile development. There is barely enough time to get the tasks of the sprint done; looking at larger architectural issues is usually the first thing to be traded off.

To make sure the wider focus is not lost, many organizations find it useful to create a separate UX stream. This stream is not part of any agile development stream—it runs in parallel to them, but synchronizes with them at key points. This stream addresses inconsistencies across the whole system and feeds fixes to those inconsistencies back into the agile development streams as new stories. This UX stream can do additional user research, design, and iteration without being tied to the particular schedule and deliverables of any one development stream. This stream maintains the whole-system coherence of the design.

4.6 PROGRAMMER/DESIGNER HOLIDAY

One of the best practices Martin, Biddle, and Noble[11] identified in the agile world is the idea of a *programmer's holiday*. Agile experts recognize that there is never enough time during focused, intense sprints to do all the architectural work and refactoring necessary to keep the code base clean and maintainable. Technical debt tends to build up over time despite the team's best efforts. They also recognize that the pace demanded by short sprints becomes exhausting over time. When you eliminate the natural down time created by project planning and field test, there is just no letup in the pace of project work.

So a programmer's holiday dedicates an iteration to code cleanup. Each developer can choose what to work on, whether refactoring a badly-implemented module, addressing bugs, or doing large-scale restructuring that affects whole subsystems.

Such a holiday can be useful to the UX team as well, especially if there is no parallel UX stream. This can be an opportunity to step back and look at the overall coherence of the UI: whether the basic structure holds up and whether it is appropriate to the user tasks. If there is a need for large-scale restructuring of the UI, affecting several screens all at the same time, this is an opportunity to do that kind of cleanup.

A team working in two-week sprints might schedule such a holiday once a quarter or so, often enough to stay on top of things but not so often that it interrupts development significantly. A team working in one-month sprints might devote half a sprint to the holiday, committing to half the normal amount of work for that sprint.

4.7 ARCHITECTURAL SPIKES FOR DIFFICULT ISSUES

Architectural spikes allow the development team to address a difficult or risky development problem. They might devote a whole sprint to studying a technology problem, prototyping alternative solutions, running load tests, and making sure that they have understood the risks and settled on an optimal solution. Such spikes happen early in development, to get the most important project risks out of the way early.

But not all project risks come from implementation concerns. Challenging UI problems may well pose as much risk to the success of a product. Consider Microsoft's ribbon interface, for example, new with *Office 7.* Would the ribbon be intuitive for new users? Would it be frustrating for experienced users? Could it present all the many functions of an *Office* product coherently? Would users get lost navigating multiple ribbons?

Use architectural spikes to address UI problems, too. When a team identifies a UI problem as a key risk, it is appropriate to devote an iteration to addressing that risk. Remember, the risk is the whole team's problem. The team can use the time to brainstorm alternatives, mock them up, and test them with users to verify that they actually work as implemented. This can be critical: not only did the ribbon have to work intuitively in theory, it had to be possible to actually put the Office products' real functions into the ribbon in a sensible way.

4.8 UX AS A FULL TEAM MEMBER

The discussion to this point has tended to treat the UX designers as separate from the development team. But one key agile principle is that everyone is on the team, and the team is co-located. Being on the team means that every team member is responsible for the success of the whole product. Everyone, including the UX designers, is a pig, not a chicken. It means that they participate in the work of implementing user stories and they are present for the daily meetings. It also means that if they are stuck or behind, it is the team's problem, not just theirs.

This principle creates a tight, cohesive team when all the team members are developers. When some team members—like UX designers—have very different skill sets, it is less obvious how to make it work well. It is easy to move around developers to address coding problems (and agile principles such as "no code ownership" are intended to make it still easier). Having a UX person help with a coding problem or having a developer help with a UI problem is more problematic.

It is also common for UX designers to be shared across multiple projects. Ideally there would be one or more UX people assigned to a project, and when the user interface is a success factor for a product, this should absolutely be the case. In the real world, the UX professional is usually juggling the demands of several projects at once.

The UX part of the organization also has its own focus that transcends individual projects: for example, developing common UI standards across the company, ensuring that the company's branding and image comes through in product UIs, ensuring that the company's UX professionals stay up to speed on the latest developments, and cross-fertilizing across UX professionals. A UX professional always has a dual allegiance: to the team they are on and to the UX community they are a part of.

Successful UX team members act like full team members. They are co-located with the team they support if at all possible. If they support multiple teams, they have a desk in each team's development room, and they do the work there as much as possible. They are present for the daily meetings unless they have a conflict; when multiple teams have their meetings at the same time, they choose which meeting to attend based on what is happening in each project. They do work based on story cards, generally, as UX tasks associated with a particular story.

As full team members, UX people can draw on the team's resources. Just as a programmer can say, "I'll need to work with a database expert for this story," the UX person can say, "I'll need someone to come with me on this paper prototyping customer visit," or even, "This is a simple, non-critical UI. Can we agree the developer will design something basic which I can just look at as a sanity check, while I spend my time on this other critical UI task?"

CHAPTER 5

Structure of a User-Centered Agile Process

Given the above best practices and what is known to work in both the user-centered and agile domains, it is possible to construct an overall approach to design and development that makes agile development truly user-centered—or, conversely, that makes user-centered development agile.

This approach makes room for coherent design by preceding agile development with a phase 0 for user research and user experience design. With a sound understanding of the user under their belt, the team can then write good user stories and go into agile development sprints confident that they know what problem they are solving and have an initial direction for solving it.

In the rest of this section, we will show how each of these parts of development can be structured to include both the UX perspective and the user iterations on which agile methods depend. For user-centered techniques, we rely on Contextual Design (CD), co-developed by the author and Karen Holtzblatt[20]. For agile techniques, we draw on the agile best practices described in Chapter 4 above and include concepts from both Scrum and XP.

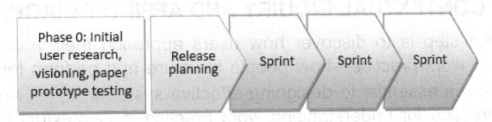

Figure 5.1: The basic structure of agile development. Coding starts when the basic goal and structure of the project is set in phase 0. This phase may be anywhere from 2-8 weeks, depending on the scope of the project.

5.1 PHASE 0: PROJECT DEFINITION

Few projects start with a completely blank slate. Existing products and systems provide the context for any new development. An existing product may need an additional feature or may need to support an additional role. The competition may have come out with a new feature, and the company may be scrambling to catch up. An internal system may need to support a redefined business process. A business may be struggling with too many standalone tools and may be looking to integrate them. (See Section 6.3 for a discussion of how to deal with larger scopes—new product development and large-scale projects.)

In each case, development starts with a general idea of the scope of the system, but so far, with no detailed agreement on the specific tasks to be supported, how those tasks are to be supported, or what the requirements on the system are. The team is not yet ready to write user stories—there is not yet agreement on what they should say, and the customer team do not yet know enough about the user to provide trustworthy guidance.

Starting the project with a phase 0 gives the team a chance to organize themselves, find out about their users, and understand the kind of solution they should build. This is the process for building the BPUF—the Big Picture Up Front—which becomes the basis for iteration during sprints.

5.1.1 CONTEXTUAL INQUIRY AND AFFINITY DIAGRAMS

The first step is to discover how users approach their work. This study of *work practice*—how people structure and perform the jobs they do—is essential to designing effective systems[21;22;23]. And the best practice for understanding work practice is Contextual Inquiry (CI).

In a Contextual Inquiry, project team members interview users in their workplaces, watching them work and talking to them about what they are doing and why. If the project is building a consumer product, the team interviews consumers in their home, cars, stores, or other life contexts, observing the life task the new product will address. At this point, the primary focus is not on design at all. The focus is on how people perform the work, what they are trying to accomplish, how they go about it, and what gets in their way.

Any kind of field research needs some training, but that is no reason for limiting this work to UX professionals. Developers and other team members can be trained to assist, and even untrained engineers can go along as observers. This supports the agile "one team" value, promotes cross-fertilization across team members, and ensures all team members understand the users' problems at a visceral level.

The contextual interview. The first principle of CI is to observe the work directly, as the user works. For traditional office work, this means going to the user's office and sitting with them, watching the user interact with online systems and with paper files and forms. The interviewer can see the informal notes and cheat sheets the user has created to help track the job and the piles the user creates to organize and stage a job. He or she can see the use of Excel to do the real organization and calculation before loading up the results into the official tool. Interruptions and informal communication happen while the interviewer is there, revealing tacit aspects of the work that might otherwise remain unarticulated. If the task requires moving around, the interviewer goes with the user, running up and down halls, driving to remote sites, crawling through access tunnels, or riding bicycles to get around a huge assembly plant (all real examples, by the way).

If the design is for a consumer product, the interview is conducted wherever the life task is performed: in the home or car, in public, while commuting or shopping.

Nor is the interviewer constrained to only the events that occur during the interview. *Retrospective accounts* give the interviewer a way to recover detailed task information about events in the recent past. Together, the interviewer and user replay a specific event of interest, using artifacts and probing questions to reveal the detailed steps of the task. In this way, the interviewer can learn about and capture the details of important tasks and situations whenever they happened, as long as it is within the recent past.

Throughout the interview, interviewer and user engage in a discussion of what the user is doing and why, and what the implications are for the project's design direction. These discussions reveal the user's intents and strategies (more tacit knowledge) that underlie their actions.

Note that the interviewer does not focus on problems and issues in the work, though those are certainly revealed in the interview. Unlike a usability test, which explicitly focuses on identifying problems, the goal of a CI is to understand the whole work practice. This understanding allows the team to envision solutions that transform the user's work rather than merely fix existing problems. For example, CIs of work practice in offices during the 1990s revealed that users tended to collect phone, calendar, rolodex, and day-timer style personal organizer together on their desks. This implied that these tasks—communication, identifying contacts, and organizing schedule and tasks—went together in the work practice. They made a natural whole. This recognition anticipated by years the introduction of combined email, address books, calendars, and task organizers in products such as Outlook.

CIs give interviewers the understanding of the users they need to represent users on the team: knowledge of the users' tasks and needs and, critically, the gut feel for what design alternatives will work for this population and what will not. Internalized knowledge and gut feel are valuable, but knowledge has to be captured and externalized if it is to be the basis of design. That is done in *interpretation sessions.*

The interpretation session. Data from any sort of field research tends to be unwieldy. The interviewer's notes are lengthy and unstructured, transcripts are difficult to create and hard to understand, and videos, if used, are cumbersome to manipulate. Interpretation sessions give the team a way to deal with field data.

In an interpretation session, the team reviews each interview by going through the interviewer's notes of the interview in detail. The interviewer retells the story of the interview from beginning to end, in order. The rest of the team captures key information which has design relevance. Individual observations are captured in a list to be printed later on sticky notes and used in the affinity. The work practice of the user is captured in work models (described in Section 5.1.3 below). By the end of the interpretation session, all important information from this user is written down and ready to be used.

From the agile perspective, it important to note that these notes (and, indeed, the affinity and work models as well) are used by the agile customer team to understand the customer. This is not an example of documentation created by one group to be passed off and consumed by another, which would be anathema to an agile team. This process enables the agile customer to understand who the user really is, what their work practice is, and consequently, what the project might do to help them.

U02-20	U02 ensures that everyone in the house knows that she is making her shopping list and that they had better get their requests to her
U04-15	Husband and wife share responsibility for tracking household needs
U07-18	U07 likes specialty stores because they carry things he can't find elsewhere, but sometimes they don't have enough turnover to keep goods from getting stale

Figure 5.2: Sample affinity notes.

5.1.2 THE AFFINITY DIAGRAM

So far, the team has focused on each user individually. But products support whole markets, not individual users. Even internal systems support roles and job positions, not the individuals who happen to be doing those jobs at the moment. So it is important for the team to be able to see the common structure of work practice, independent of individual users without losing the variation that exists across users.

Affinity diagrams have come to be widely used as a method for organizing large amounts of unstructured data. An affinity diagram is built from the user data collected through CI and it reveals key issues across all users studied: key elements of the work practice, user objectives and how they are achieved, pain points, workarounds, tools used, and so forth. The team builds an affinity from their observations after interviewing users.

An affinity is built from the bottom up by first grouping similar observations, labeling them, then building larger groups out of these small groups. It is not built by starting with large classifications or by sorting notes into predefined categories. The result is that the structure of an affinity reflects the weight of the data, with less influence coming from the team's preconceived ideas. This is essential to push insight; the team discovers new ideas and perspectives by how the data comes together.

An affinity can be built by the team in one or two days.

5.1.3 WORK MODELING

The affinity collects and organizes issues across all users studied, but it does not show the structure of work practice coherently. There is no place on the affinity wall that does a task analysis, for example —that shows the steps users perform to accomplish a task. There is no organized representation of the physical environment where the work happens, or the artifacts people use to accomplish it.

Work models are the appropriate tool to show the structure of work practice. They drive design thinking by suggesting how different design approaches will or will not support the work. Work models are built during the interpretation sessions from the data collected in Contextual Inquiries. Like the affinity, they are consolidated across users to show the common structure of work.

Figure 5.3: A section of an affinity showing how individual observations (the yellow stickies) are grouped to reveal design implications. Photographs taken during interviews may also be incorporated into the affinity.

Contextual Design defines five types of work models, but phase 0 for an agile project usually depends primarily on sequence models. That is because the larger context of the project has already been defined through marketing research, business process redesign, or existing systems that are being revised. Models that help to understand the larger context are not needed in a more focused project. (If your project is not so focused, *Contextual Design*[20] describes all the models and how to do concepting and ideation in a user-centered way.)

The sequence model. Specific tasks are analyzed and represented with sequence models, and nearly every project will want to build them. Sequence models show the common structure of each relevant task users perform. They show the high-level structure of the task, the different strategies used, intents the users are trying to achieve, and the problems getting in the way of the work.

Sequence models are built from current work practice, but their importance is precisely because they help keep designers from getting stuck in the current way of doing things. Incremental development runs the risk of focusing on incremental fixes, eliminating pain points one by one without ever looking at the overall structure of the task or thinking about a radical redesign of how it is supported.

Sequence models show the many tedious steps required to achieve a user's intent. They show how different strategies imply different intents and suggest how a different approach in the system would allow users to achieve their intents more directly. They show how whole tasks have been created merely to overcome system constraints and suggest how those tasks might be eliminated. By looking at the whole task together, they move the team from thinking about point fixes to systemic solutions.

Sequence 1: Monitoring incoming customer email

U1-1-1   Intent: Be sure priority customers and sales opportunities are handled quickly

U1-1-2   Trigger: Realize that mail hasn't been checked over an hour

U1-1-3   Go to tech service mail box and scan the senders and subjects

U1-1-4   Set priorities for how to work through the email

U1-1-5   See a request for a recommendation for replacement part

...

Figure 5.4: A partial sequence model showing how the steps of the sequence are captured. Only the exact steps done by this user when this particular event occurred are recorded.

The artifact model. People create artifacts to help them do their work. They may keep a list of contact numbers on a piece of paper by their computer; they may use a spreadsheet to calculate discounts and then circumvent the tool in the system that is supposed to calculate discounts for them. Each artifact offers insight into how the user approaches their work and what they need to support it. Each artifact offers details for how to get that support right: Exactly what information does the user keep for each contact? How are they calculating the discount, and how is that different from what the system would have done?

When artifacts are important to the users' work, it may be useful to capture them. Sometimes an artifact suggests that the system must do something and do it a certain way, such as calculate a discount a certain way. Other artifacts provide the exact details needed to implement a story, such as the specific contact information needed by users. Even if the details are not written into the story—and since stories are high-level, they may not be—developers will come asking what to do in the implementation and the UX designer needs to be ready with an answer.

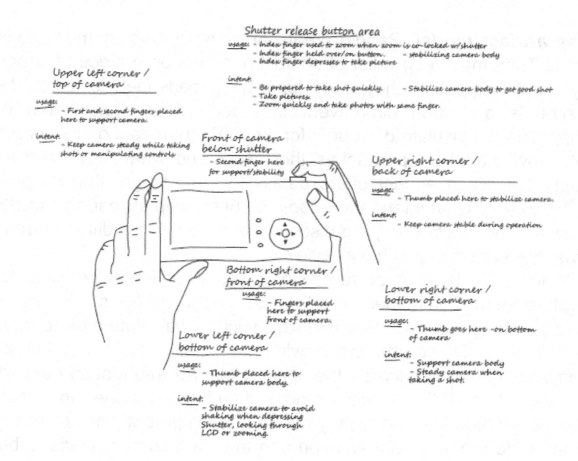

Figure 5.5: An artifact model showing the important aspects of the artifact (a digital camera) and information about how it is used.

5.1.4 PERSONAS

Personas are a popular way of representing a project's user population. Unlike affinity and work models, which give the team a way to see the structure of their users' work, personas are primarily a communication mechanism to give stakeholders insight into who the users are. As such, they break the agile value of "no documentation for the sake of documentation," yet teams have found them so useful as a concrete touchstone for understanding their users that it is often worthwhile to create them.

Personas are characterizations of the different types of users as though they were real individuals. In projects operating without a good grounding in user research, personas are built by capturing stakeholders' impressions of who their customers are. But when a project has started with extensive user research, as outlined above, personas can and should be based on the actual users studied.

Since no actual individual is a perfect characterization of a type, information from actual users is combined to produce a single persona. Those aspects of the persona which are common and relevant are collected from different actual users to present a full picture of the persona. At the same time, details which are idiosyncratic or distracting are left out.

Personas can be used to ground communication throughout development. Initially, user stories can be written to support the specific personas: "As Anna, the lightweight project manager, I want to..." During iterations, referring to specific personas reminds the team of how roles, tasks, and attitudes combine in real people to ensure the design takes all a user's needs into account. Because personas are written as though the people are real, they are easy to deal with. They do not appear to be an abstraction.

Al Johnson, Reluctant HR Expert

"We think we are a modern employer"

Al Johnson is the finance director at a small manufacturing firm. He'd really prefer to spend 100% of his time overseeing finances and operations but he usually needs to devote almost half his time to HR issues. He's not trained for it and has no particular HR expertise, and the laws are so complex that though they try to treat their people well, Al constantly worries about whether his firm is at risk. He tries to keep on top of the latest updates in HR law and regulations, but there's so much information it's easy to miss things.

Goals

- Focus on his "real job" of finance and operations, minimizing time spent on HR work
- Make sure his firm is not at risk because of how they treat employee issues
- Make a good employment environment for his people
- Stay on top of the "right way" to execute HR tasks

Al Johnson's time is stretched thin at his small manufacturing firm. Not only is he its full-time financial director, he's also the only one who can act as an HR expert in the firm. As a result, he is forced into the position of working on HR issues for which he is ill-trained.

Recently, for example, an employee got sick just before a planned vacation. Does his time out qualify as sick leave or vacation time? Another employee wanted to take vacation right before her maternity leave started, leaving a big hole in the staffing of this small firm. Should this request be honored?

And yet the firm wants to treat their employees well. For example, they have generous flex-time policies and participate in Britain's bike-to-work program. Al worked extra hard to make sure the pregnant employee, a recent Iraqi immigrant, understood the process and her rights.

Keeping on top of HR law and best practices is an ongoing headache for Al. He subscribes to an HR news services, but they send much too much information and very little of it is relevant to his specific situation. It is easy to miss important issues—it was his factory manager who noticed and told Al about the last increase in minimum pay.

Al does work with an external HR firm to augment his own knowledge. But he often doesn't think to bring them into a problem right at the beginning, which reduces their effectiveness.

Tasks

- Oversee HR processes: Hiring, firing, discipline, and other employee issues
- Review proposed employee policies to ensure they meet HR regulatory requirements
- Work with external HR experts on handling specific issues
- Track employee absence, vacations, and sick leave

Roles

- Finance Operations Overseer
- Regulation Compliance Ensurer
- Disciplinary Process Manager
- Dismissal Process Manager
- HR Documents Maintainer

Figure 5.6: A persona. All the details in this persona are actual data from customer interviews.

5.1.5 VISIONING

Creating a system vision—a high-level concept of what the system is to do—is a necessary precursor to writing user stories. To see why, consider a typical story that might be written to support a network monitor role: "As a network monitor, I want to see a warning when a communications line reaches 90% of capacity so I can prevent network outages or slowdowns."

"No," someone might say. "The system should rebalance network traffic on its own."

"No," another team member might reply. "I don't think the system can do that. But we shouldn't bother the network monitor with warnings they can't do anything about. They'll be overwhelmed."

Who is right? The traditional answer from agile methods is: the agile customer or the product owner, and the team should defer to them. But that is not good enough for us. We need to say *how* those roles develop the understanding so that they can give an accurate, trustworthy answer. As we showed above, the people representing users to the team are rarely the actual end-user. Even if they were, end-users themselves might not know how to give a trustworthy answer. How should they know if they would be overwhelmed or not?

In the section on paper prototyping (Section 5.1.8 below), we will take up the question of how to decide what the right answer is. For now, notice that each speaker has a very different idea of what the system should do, how it should be structured, and how extensive the support it provides users should be. Should the system be automatic, doing much of the work for the operators, or not? Should we expect the users to be sitting in front of a screen all day looking for problems, or will they be distracted with other work?

These are the basic questions that define the system—its scope, its desired impact on the work practice, the basic function and structure to be provided, and the details of its behavior—and they need to be resolved before release planning. Often they are not, and the result is that the release planning meeting is not just about writing story cards. Participants have to design the whole system, in their heads, with no process support and no way to see the whole thing at once, and then write the results of their implicit design on story cards. This makes for a difficult meeting.

Instead, the BPUF (Big Picture Up Front) best practice suggests going into release planning after first sketching out an overall understanding of what the system is and what it is to do. The Contextual Design way to do this is with a *product vision* built together as a team, after collecting and analyzing user data with contextual inquiries, building an affinity, and creating work models.

A vision is built cooperatively by the whole team, including the product owner, UX designers, and developers. The only constraint is that everyone in the vision must also "walk the data:" review the data in detail and together. This is necessary to ensure that everyone's ideas respond to the actual user data, rather than just repeating their own prejudices and misconceptions.

The vision, itself, is drawn on a flip chart, written in pen. The team describes how the user will do their work in the context of the new system, inventing features as they go to improve the work process. They naturally structure the system into coherent parts, each supporting a set of end-users (often referring to personas) and a set of work tasks. As in a brainstorm, the team does not evaluate while visioning; any problems are overcome through further visioning.

A team will always do several visions, exploring different approaches to the problem. Then the team can evaluate. They look at each vision in turn, decide what works and what does not about each vision, and then consolidate the visions, eliminating those aspects that are infeasible or unnecessary, and bringing together the parts that work into a single, coherent view of the system.

This visioning process fits well into the agile approach and mindset. It is a quick process. Visioning can be done in one to three days, depending on the scope of the project and the number of visions. The documentation created is exactly the documentation needed by the team to do the work: the drawing of the vision on the flip chart. And letting the vision be hand-drawn ensures that it remains a sketch—a big picture—and keeps the team from over-focusing on the details.

5.1.6 STORYBOARDS

It is possible to write user stories directly from the vision. Each element of the vision can be captured in one or more user stories, which can be prioritized and used to drive agile development. But the vision itself has not yet been validated. Any stories based on the vision will need to be tested and iterated with users, usually needing several iterations to get it right. The lag between creating the vision and testing it, possibly many sprints later, will be long.

It is better to test and iterate the vision with users right away. This puts off the start of agile development but ensures that the initial stories reflect users' real needs. Less rework will be needed during sprints to respond to users' feedback.

In Contextual Design, the vision concept is tested by mocking it up in paper and iterating it with users. Users can respond effectively to a concrete user interface; it is much harder for them to respond to an abstract concept. A quick, high-level user interface design provides a concrete representation of the vision that acts as a communication device between designers and users. Detailed UI design can safely be put off until the development sprints.

However, jumping directly from the vision to UI design can leave holes. The task flow in the new system must be coherent and convenient for users. Unless task support is designed directly, some activities may not be supported or some sequences of steps may not flow well in the system. These problems will be discovered and fixed during prototyping iterations, but that is a slower and more cumbersome process than getting them right up front. Storyboards help the team discover and fix such problems sooner.

A storyboard lays out how the user accomplishes a specific task in the proposed system. Like laying out a storyboard for a movie, each storyboard cell shows how a step in the task is done. It shows the users involved, the UI screens they interact with, the data that appears on those screens, the actions they take, and any system behavior that is triggered by the user's actions or by other events. Each storyboard ensures that the task is coherent, that it can be performed smoothly and efficiently from start to finish, and that it takes into account any human processes, offline systems, and external systems the user may have to use along the way.

Each storyboard covers a single task and case. For example, a storyboard might show how the people monitoring a network are alerted to and respond to an emergency such as a power outage. Another storyboard might show how they would respond to a different kind of emergency, such as a hacker attack, which would exercise different elements of the system. Other storyboards would cover other tasks. Usually 6-12 storyboards are enough to cover the main work practice of a typical system. A storyboard typically takes no more than a few hours to create.

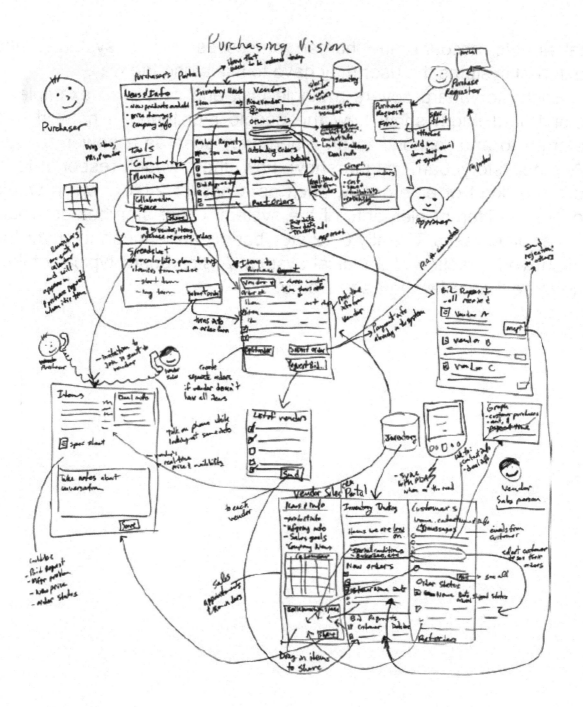

Figure 5.7: A vision: hand-drawn in a short interactive session with the team. It shows how users interact with the new system and do work outside it to accomplish their tasks.

Figure 5.8: A storyboard, showing how the interaction between user and system is represented. (A camera is being designed in this storyboard.)

5.1.7 USER ENVIRONMENT DESIGN

Storyboards keep specific tasks coherent, ensuring that it is possible to go from step to step of the task in the system. But thinking only about individual tasks tends to create systems that are collections of wizards, each focused on supporting one task one way. Good systems are like houses: collections of rooms or spaces, each supporting a range of activities, each connected to other spaces in the house in ways that make sense for the work people do. Houses support many life tasks, many unforeseen by the architect; good systems do the same.

The User Environment Design (UED) gives the Customer Team a way to represent, at a high level, the structure of the system as experienced by the user. It does not show details of appearance or implementation; instead, it just shows the places in the system and how they connect. It is like a floor plan for a software system or the site map for a web site.

Focus Areas are the places in a UED. Like the rooms of a house, they are experienced as a coherent place. They will be implemented as a coherent part of the UI such as a screen, page, or pane. Each Focus Area has a purpose, the work that it is intended to support. Each Focus Area provides function, describing what the system shows and does for the user in that place and what commands the place makes available to the user to invoke system behavior. In addition, each Focus Area provides access to other Focus Areas, allowing the user to move through the system.

Building a UED for a typical agile project takes 2-3 days.

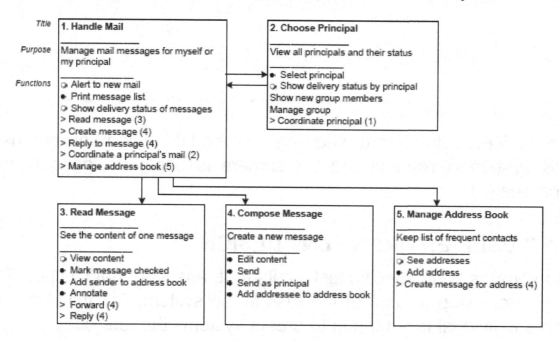

Figure 5.9: A partial UED showing the core of an email system.

5.1.8 PAPER PROTOTYPING

A key problem for any sort of user-centered design, including agile methods, is how to get accurate feedback from users. Users are not designers. They do not normally articulate their work practice and cannot envision how a proposed change would affect them on a day-to-day basis. How can they know how to advise the development team? An agile process allows the team to do the wrong thing and fix it more quickly—but we would like to do the right thing in the first place.

Paper prototyping provides an answer that has been widely and successfully used[24]. Rather than describe a solution, show it. Rather than ask users how they like it, ask them to work with it. Rather than give them a task to do, ask them to do their own task in the prototyped system.

Prototyping can validate the system concept—that it is something people want, can refine the overall structure of the system, can ensure that the right functions are provided, and can refine the detailed behavior of individual functions. The prototype represents the system as a whole, so it helps to keep the design coherent across the system. User stories tend to break the system into independent bits, so this coherent view is especially important to maintain in an agile project.

Paper prototypes are quick to build. A designer can have a simple UI mocked up in half a day or so. Paper is easy to transport and, once at the user's workplace, easy to work with. Paper prototypes are also easy to modify. When user or designer suggests a change, they can mock up the change and put it into the prototype immediately. The user can experience it and decide whether they like it as well as they thought they would.

A paper prototyping session is run as a partnership between the designer and user. The first thing the designer does is find out about the details of the user's work and modify the prototype so that it represents the user's own data and situation. By using their own known information as clues for how the system is structured, the user can respond to it as though it were real, Therefore, they can pursue their own work tasks in the system, with the designer bringing out new system elements as needed. When there is a glitch, user and designer discuss the problem and decide together on a fix, which they implement (in paper) immediately.

Paper prototyping is done at two stages in an agile process: first, during phase 0, paper prototyping is used to validate the vision. Any vision represents a guess on the part of the team—a good guess, based on data, but a guess nonetheless. By mocking it up and testing it in paper, the team can reduce the lag between the time the design was created (the visioning session) and when it was validated by users. Two rounds of paper prototyping are enough to give the team the confidence that the stories they write are reasonable and valuable solutions to user problems.

However, paper prototypes and user stories alike are rough, high-level descriptions of solutions. They do not specify exactly how an interface will look or the detailed layout and interaction. Nor, by agile principles, should they. YAGNI (You Ain't Gonna Need It) advises that if you design too far ahead, you are likely to design features that will never be used. So instead, the detailed design is done immediately before implementation, using the best practice of designing one sprint ahead of implementation. That gives the UX designers enough time to work out and iterate the details with users before the developers come asking how a story is to be done. This UI testing is also done with paper prototypes, which are now more highly rendered, closer to the actual UI. If two rounds of prototyping were done during phase 0, a single round of prototyping is generally enough during sprints.

5.2 THE RELEASE PLANNING SESSION

Agile development starts with a release planning session. Together, but driven by the product owner or customer representative, the team writes user stories to represent the key elements of the release. UX designers and others who participated in user research during phase 0 with them act as the customer representative. They should act directly in that role on the team, and support the product owner with their knowledge of user work practice.

5.2.1 WRITING USER STORIES

Each user story captures an element or feature of the design. Stories are written on cards for the same reason that visions are written on flip charts: to keep the team from over-specifying and over-designing. All that will fit on a card is a simple, high-level description of the function or behavior.

The team writes stories by walking through their design (as represented by their vision, UED, or prototype), identifying each design element, and writing a story card to capture that element. A user story should provide value to the user; if several functions work together to provide desired user behavior, they may grouped into a single user story.

User stories are written from the user's point of view to emphasize the value that the card will deliver. Take the example user story, "As a network monitor, I want to see a warning when a communications line reaches 90% of capacity, so I can prevent network outages or slowdowns." This specifies the feature, ties it to value, and specifies which users will be supported by the card. It does not specify every detail: how the warning is to be delivered, whether the warning will be delivered no matter what the user is currently doing, or how to show the warning so users have enough context to interpret it immediately.

The level of detail written in the card depends to some degree on the confidence of the UX designers. The number 90%, for example, indicates that the designers believe, based on their iterations with users, that 90% is the right threshold. If they were less confident or less specific in their knowledge they might leave the precise threshold open, to be determined later through additional customer work. Either way, inquiries and testing with customers may change the threshold once this card is selected for implementation.

Story cards are intended to deliver practical user value, and also to be entirely implemented within a single sprint. This means that complex functions will be split across several stories so that each is small enough to fit in a sprint. This is to be expected. It may well be that the part of the function specified on a single card may not be in itself enough to *satisfy* users, but it should be complete and implementable by itself.

Returning to our example, the initial story card might specify only that the warning must be given, no matter how. The implementation team would be expected to implement it in the simplest fashion possible, getting the underlying mechanism in place but with no effort expended in the user presentation. The team might implement a simple alert box.

Additional story cards would be written to complete the function. One might specify a visual icon to appear on the network map. Another might specify that hovering over that icon reveals additional details. Another, that clicking on the icon would bring up a troubleshooting tool. Another, that when the network map is not visible a sliding pane will fade in and after a moment fade out in the lower-right corner of the screen. Each story is separately implementable and separately testable (though all depend on the initial story being implemented first).

Implementation teams new to agile development may find this approach awkward. It requires that they revisit the same function and same section of code several times over several sprints. This runs counter to traditional development practice. Traditionally, developers would want to implement all related functionality at once, create, get into, and get out of that module, and not have to revisit it later in development.

The upside of the agile approach to implementation is flexibility and predictability. Each story is small enough to be reliably estimated; if the estimation is off, since the story is small, it will be off by hours or a few days, not by weeks or months. And it allows the team to change course. For example, if it turns out that, once implemented, users like the network map so well that they leave it up all the time, the story about showing alerts in a separate pane might not need to be implemented at all. The time this story would have taken to implement can be allotted to other, more important stories.

5.2.2 ESTIMATING COST

As story cards are written, the team estimates the cost of implementing them. This may be done in "ideal programmer days," the number of days a programmer would take if they had no interruptions and could concentrate only on this one task. This is a useful way for a new team to start with estimating stories. By referring back to real (if ideal) time, the team has a conceptual framework for assigning a number.

But experienced teams often find it more convenient to assign "points" to stories. A point has no unit, no real-world reference. But a story estimated at 4 points can be implemented in half the length of time required for a story of 8 points, and it will take twice as long as a 2-point story. An experienced team has estimated and implemented enough stories so that they can look at a new one and score it by comparing it with work they have done in the past.

Again, this seems odd from the perspective of traditional development. It works in agile teams because they measure progress in terms of *velocity:* the number of story points the team can implement in a single sprint. That number is tracked from sprint to sprint and the team assumes it will not change by much next time round. The team commits to implement specific stories in an iteration, and as long as the points for those stories add up to no more than their velocity, the team can be reasonably confident they can get all the stories done.

A brand new team, of course, has no measure of velocity to go on. For such a team, estimating by ideal programmer days for the first few iterations lets them use their gut feel to come up with a reasonable number. Velocity can be initially estimated by taking the total programmer-days available in an iteration and scaling back in the usual way to account for meetings and overhead. After a few iterations, the team's measured velocity can take over.

UX designers should be ready to discuss the implementation cost of UI design. Remember that the cost includes all work not yet done to finish the story, including work to be done by the UX team. So a story card that refers to a complex part of the UI needing extensive UX work should have that work factored into its implementation cost.

5.2.3 PLANNING THE RELEASE

Once stories are written and estimated, they can be organized into sprints. Each sprint needs to make sense in several possibly conflicting ways. It should be implementable, which implies that if other stories implement necessary features or underlying modules, they should be scheduled first. Each sprint should support user testing, providing a coherent user interface. Risky stories depending on unknown or tricky technology should be implemented early so the risk can be eliminated or mitigated as soon as possible. High-priority stories, the ones most important to customer and stakeholders, should be implemented early.

In addition, of course, the total story points of each sprint must be less than the velocity. In fact, the team should allow a buffer of 20% or so in sprints following sprint 1, or else plan regular programmer's holidays. There will be bugs to fix; there will be rework to do in response to user feedback. If this time is not planned from the beginning, it will cause chaos later in the process. Either there will need to be extensive reprioritization at each sprint planning session to incorporate rework into the development stream, or the rework will be put off (increasing technical debt), or the team will have to overwork.

It is often useful for a sprint to have an organizing theme: a sprint might implement all monitoring with a bare-bones UI or might provide remote access throughout the system.

The first two sprints should be planned carefully, with the exact stories chosen. The following sprints can be organized more roughly. Careful planning of the entire release is generally counterproductive; too much might change before later sprints are started. Therefore, once users have experienced initial baselevels, the priority of following stories has a possibility to change: the business might change direction, rebalancing priorities or changing the delivery date; or the velocity of the team might change.

The release is a trade-off between function and date. Each sprint takes a fixed, known time; the velocity is known or estimated and determines the number of story points in each sprint. Therefore, the team can calculate how many sprints will be needed to deliver the critical function for the release. That sets the release date. UX designers should be prepared to argue for features to include in the release to support users' work practice. The business and marketing people may have requirements for what must be in the release for business reasons, and those are legitimate considerations. But it is the UX designers (and any other team members who gathered data with them) who understand the real impact of the proposed system on the end-users.

The release date can be adjusted by moving stories between releases; where a function has been split across stories, the stories that make the function more elaborate might be moved out of the release altogether to make room for more important stories. What must not happen is to jam more stories into the sprints. This is a hard discipline for newly agile organizations. The traditional dynamic often has management pushing developers to "do more," insisting on an unrealistic delivery date for business reasons. The agile tools help reveal that this is planning that creates chaos: it is planning for the team to execute at a speed the team knows and can demonstrate it cannot achieve.

This release plan should not be taken as cast in stone. It shows how the team can deliver certain functionality by a certain date, but it is expected that as the team learns more about its users and as users learn more about how the new system will affect their work, the plan will change. Each sprint planning session may change story priorities, rewrite stories, and introduce new stories. This is expected, and one of the reasons agile teams deliver useful results.

If any stories are critical to the business for external reasons, it is up to the team to know and represent those constraints. The team is in close contact with its users via continual testing and feedback. Any adjustments the team makes along the way should meet user needs more precisely. On the other hand, management may have made commitments to important customers. Product marketing may feel that the product must have a certain feature to compete in the marketplace, whether or not that feature is actually useful. (This happens more often than you might think.) Or other parts of the organization—manufacturing, or training—might be gearing up in parallel, expecting and depending on certain features to be present. Such commitments to stakeholders other than the end-user must be understood by the team, so they can be honored.

5.3 RUNNING SPRINTS

With the release plan in place, agile development proceeds in a series of sprints. Each sprint implements a set of user stories. Where these stories define user interaction, the visual design has not yet been done—rough wireframes and paper prototypes are enough to test the concept. Any further design is put off until needed.

To give the UX designers time to develop final UIs and test them with users, the best practice is to work one sprint ahead of developers and test one sprint behind. So in sprint 1, the UI people develop and test the final screen appearance for a user story; in sprint 2, they work with development to implement it; and in sprint 3, they test the implementation to ensure nothing was lost in the translation.

The first sprint may be treated specially. Often, there is a fair amount of work necessary to get the team up to speed. On the implementation side, such activities include defining the development practices, putting together an automated build and test mechanism, and deciding on and implementing a source code control system. On the UX side, there are detailed interaction designs and final visual designs to work out and test for the initial user stories. So, the first sprint may not deliver actual user value, but it may put all the building blocks in place for the project. This is especially important for a new team that has to set up its tools and procedures for the first time. It is also important for the UX team, who need to provide detailed visual designs to developers before the developers start coding.

Table 5.1: The UX work on a story interleaves with development of the story, with design done one sprint ahead of implementation and user testing one sprint behind.

	UXTeam	Development Team
Sprint 1	Design UI for story 1;	Put development system in

	prototype and iterate with users	place; implement low-UI stories
Sprint 2	Design & iterate UI for story 2 Consult on implementation of story 1	Implement story 1
Sprint 3	Test implementation of story 1 with end-users Consult on implementation of story 2 Design & iterate UI for story 3	Implement story 2

Once the team is in the swing of iterative development, they repeat the same pattern over and over again, as follows.

5.3.1 SPRINT PLANNING

The team meets to plan the work for the sprint. This starts with the set of stories identified during release planning, but this is the time to consider whether that plan still makes sense. Do these stories still reflect the next most important, useful, and risky set of stories remaining to do? Is there other work, unforeseen when the project started, that should be planned? In that case, stories need to be written, estimated, and prioritized into the schedule. Is there rework to do, either bugs to fix or redesigns to implement, based on user feedback? Then stories need to be written and prioritized into the schedule. The specific stories for the current and the next sprint need to be determined.

Then most teams will write *task cards* for each of the stories in the current implementation. It is a useful discipline to mandate that no one does work unless it is to implement a task card. (And task cards are only created to implement user stories, so all work provides customer value.) Task cards can represent implementation tasks, such as, writing code and designing databases. They can represent UX tasks: user tests, paper prototypes, and UI design. They can represent tasks to be performed by other members of the team, such as documentation and QA.

The UX team needs task cards for the stories in the last, the current, and the next sprints. Their task cards for stories in the current sprint specify UI design tasks: doing low-level layout and visual design to support developers before they start coding the story.

But the UX team also needs to look ahead to the next sprint. They write task cards to start UI design on those stories: taking the high-level design from vision, storyboards, and UED, and designing the final layout and look for this UI. If several paper prototype rounds were done in phase 0, they may design and test the finished UI directly; otherwise, they may need one or two rounds of paper prototypes first. These designs are tested with users during the current sprint for implementation in the next.

And the UX team also writes tasks for the work completed in the last sprint, to take working code and test it with users to ensure the final implementation actually works for people.

5.3.2 WORKING WITHDEVELOPMENT

During the sprint, developers implement stories. The UX team has three jobs running in parallel reflected in the three types of task cards. First, they support the developers. They provide detailed UI designs and consult with developers on detailed behavior and look. Remember, in an agile team, these consultations are where the real decisions are made and the detailed behavior is communicated. There is no functional specification; UX designers work with the developer during the sprint to say exactly what they want. It is up to the UX people to be tightly tied into the development team, providing guidance and answering questions as they come up. Daily discussions between developers and UX designers are usual.

The UX team also runs customer visits throughout the iteration to bring real user feedback into the development process. These visits accomplish the dual purpose of testing work done in the previous iteration and doing low-level design for work to be done in the next iteration. The team does this by running a customer interview that combines contextual inquiry and paper prototyping.

5.3.3 SPRINT INTERVIEW PREPARATION

Before the interview, UX team members identify which elements of the work done in the prior sprint need user feedback. Ideally, all UIs would be tested with users; in practice, teams are often making trade-offs in the use of limited resources. If a UI is straightforward or similar to what users have now, the team might decide that it is not sufficiently important to spend time on. But parts of the UI which are new, tricky, introduce new interaction paradigms, or depend on the exact behavior or look of the UI elements should be tested in the running code. For these parts of the UI, this is where the rubber hits the road: does the implementation conform well enough to the design that it actually works as expected? Or did the translation to running code introduce enough glitches or changes that usability of the system is affected?

The UX team also looks at the stories to be implemented in the next sprint and evaluates where the trouble spots are. Which stories implement UIs that were not thoroughly tested, or that could not be well prototyped in paper because they are too interactive, or that depend strongly on the detailed visual design for success or failure? Or are they new stories for user tasks which were not covered by the initial research at all? The UI design for these stories will need to be started and tested with users before the next sprint starts.

To test the UI for these stories, the UX team develops the final, fully-rendered visual design and then chooses how to prototype it with users. If interactivity is not a problem, they may print the rendered UIs and show them to users on paper. Otherwise, they build a more or less complex online prototype ranging from a simple flat image to a fully interactive prototype. Remember, this is a team responsibility. It is reasonable to collaborate with a developer to build a more interactive prototype than the UX team member could build on their own. That is just part of the cost of the story.

5.3.4 THE SPRINT INTERVIEW

The interview is run as follows: The interviewer introduces themselves and their focus to the user. They tell the user which elements of the system they want to test and what tasks the prototype supports. Then the interviewer gets an overview of the user's work, enough to get oriented and understand how to introduce the prototype. During this initial introduction, the interviewer plans how they will run the interview and what they will cover.

If the team needs to test a new design, the interviewer goes into paper prototyping mode. Sometimes the prototype really will be in paper, though more detailed and exact than the prototypes developed during phase 0. If so, the interviewing process is similar: walk through the user's own real-world examples, discuss how the prototype supports the user in doing the work, revise and modify it on the fly as problems are discovered. An online prototype, of course, is less flexible. But the interview still follows specific past events, replaying them using the prototype system. Interviewer and user discuss any issues and how they might be fixed. The interviewer can sketch solutions if significant changes are being made.

If the team needs to test parts of the previous iteration, they make the running code available, either on a laptop or through a web interface. The interviewer brings up the code for the user and then proceeds as for an online prototype except that now the interaction is real. The user interacts directly with the system, getting a feel for such issues as lag time, ability to recognize UI elements, interactivity, and so forth.

It is possible that the team needs to understand a work task, either because it is new to the team or because they need additional detail. If the user does the task, the interviewer moves into CI mode. Using observation of ongoing work and inquiry to build retrospective accounts, the interviewer discovers how the task has been done by this user. This data is captured in the interviewer's notes for interpretation and analysis by the team in a later interpretation session.

A typical session may incorporate all three styles of interview. The interview should be planned for two hours, which is enough time to investigate a range of issues but not so much that it becomes hard to get users to commit the time.

5.3.5 THE INTERPRETATION SESSION

As with CIs and paper prototype interviews, the data from the interview is analyzed in an interpretation session. The UX team and any part of the full project team that is interested goes through the events of the interview, in order. The team writes notes to capture issues and also validations.

Afterwards, the team evaluates the results of the session. Any notes about a proposed design—a design for a story that has not yet been implemented—are used to change the design and, eventually, produce a revised prototype. Notes identifying issues in the last sprint are more complicated. The team redesigns the interface to solve the problem and writes a story card to represent that fix. The story card will be prioritized in the next sprint planning session.

This is the preferred method of handling rework. Some teams prefer to do rework through the bug fix process, treating UI problems as bugs to fix. This can work, but tends to bury UI problems with the rest of the bugs, and it breaks the rule of doing no work without a user story to justify it. In truth, large bug lists are a danger sign on an agile project. They represent technical debt; worse, any priority 1 bugs on the list mean that the system is not, in fact, ready to ship at the end of the sprint. It is better to prioritize fixing them into the next sprint, even if other user stories have to be put off. And it is better not to add to them with UI changes that could be handled through the user story process.

Note that this way of working requires continual customer visits throughout the sprints.This is inevitable if user feedback is to drive iterative change. An effective customer team will have someone charged with recruiting users and planning visits. Many teams find it simplest to plan these visits ahead of time, on one or two fixed days of the week. Then, rather than scrambling to set up a user visit once they have something to test, the team scrambles to finish their prototypes in time for the next visit. The first approach creates delay waiting for users to respond and arrangements to be finalized. The second encourages progress, as designers work to get enough in place to make the visit productive.

CHAPTER 6

Structuring Projects

In this final section, we discuss typical project situations and how they might appropriately be handled. We start with simpler situations and work back up to the large, complex projects.

6.1 JUMPING ON A MOVING TRAIN

UX practitioners are likely to find themselves dropped into a project that is already using an agile methodology. The team may have at least a few sprints under their belt and may be following agile methods more or less faithfully. The challenge for the UX practitioner is to help them improve how they work with their customers and better integrate the UX work.

In this case, it is neither possible nor desirable to stop and do all the pre-work of phase 0. Instead, UX designers should move towards greater user involvement through a series of steps, without disrupting ongoing development.

1. **Do User Tests in the Users'Workplace.** If the team is not currently working directly with actual end-users, start setting up field visits with users. Arrange them so that you can see users do real work and understand the real work context. These visits can be planned ahead, as discussed above, and the exact focus of the interview adjusted to reflect project needs.

   Initially, use the interviews to prototype UIs that will be needed in this sprint or the next, so that the user data directly informs the development process. This makes them easier to justify to a possibly skeptical team and management: "We've planned this story into this sprint. I want to test it out with customers to get the UI details right."

If the team currently brings users in to test product iterations, move at least some of these sessions out to the field. Use the customer visits to run hybrid interviews, where part of the visit supports detailed design of new UIs and part provides user test and feedback of completed implementations.

2. **Work Towards Designing a Sprint Ahead.** Look at the stories to be implemented in the next sprint, according to the release plan. Start work on the UX design for those stories. Mock them up and get some user feedback before the sprint starts. If a design is well thought out, make your prototype detailed and test the look and interaction; if it is a new design for a task you understand less well, make a rough prototype and test the basic concept and function. Spend part of the interview getting feedback on paper prototypes of stories for the next sprint and part getting feedback on stories for the current sprint. Since users' work hangs together —it is not split into neat little boxes, as user stories are—this is natural and easy to do.

3. **Start Gathering Work Practice Data.** Typically, organizations collect two kinds of user data: marketing requirements of wish lists and desires and the results of usability tests. Once field interviews are happening, the team can start collecting actual work practice data. Start with observational notes and sequence models for tasks of interest to the project. These are straightforward to capture and can be quickly consolidated. Use the initial part of the interview as a more general CI to capture this data; then move into a feedback session on the design or implementation to be tested.

4. **Use a Project Break to Step Back.** After collecting work practice data during a few iterations, the UX team will have enough to be worth stepping back and evaluating the overall direction of the project compared with the needs of the users. Either between releases or during a programmer's holiday, consolidate the work practice data, building models and an affinity diagram. Build a User Environment Design of the system as implemented to date

and extend it using the stories not yet implemented. Walk through the data and UED, to identify where the project is failing to address important work issues or where the proposed implementation seems problematic. The UX team designs fixes, tests them with users (perhaps using rough paper prototyping), and writes stories to capture these changes.

6.2 SYSTEM EXTENSION

When an existing product or system is being extended with new features, a phase 0 gives the team the opportunity to learn about the new tasks to be supported: how they are structured, what strategies users adopt, and what issues get in their way? Contextual interviews and sequence models help the team gain this understanding.

Example 6.1 Typical problem statements extending an existing system to cover a new task, to add a new feature set, or to implement a new technology.

"Users need to track and report metrics in our call center tool."

"Users need to be able to save searches, and use searches to set up alerts in our information library."

"Users need to organize and track their research as a project."

The team conducts interviews with users performing the task using their current method, with whatever technology they have. During interpretation sessions, the team captures sequence models as well as notes for the affinity and consolidates sequence models to represent the task.

This coherent view of the task leads to design insight. It leads the team to understand how the task as a whole can be better supported and how different approaches in the system can help users achieve their goals more directly. The team (including the UX designers, developers, and interested stakeholders) conducts a visioning session to explore the different options and settle on a single approach.

Because this is a new task, it is likely to need new user interfaces to support it, rather than simple fixes to existing interfaces. These new interfaces are designed and tested using paper prototypes. Since they are new, designers cannot assume they are just about right the first time, so doing a few rounds of paper prototypes with users before iterative development starts ensures that the team has truly understood the user needs and has a workable solution. User stories are written based on the vision and final prototypes.

This process works when there are a small number of tasks to support (1-3), and a limited set of user roles doing those tasks (1-4). Interviews need to be run with at least three representatives of each role to understand the range of approaches to the task.

6.3 MAJOR NEW RELEASE

When a project is planning a new product or release with significant new function, the project should start with a strategic design to understand the domain and envision an overall solution. Such a project may make a significant change to work practice, may design whole new systems and interfaces, and may affect several roles and tasks. In this case, the limited scope of a phase 0 is not enough to understand the market, the problem domain, and the range of potential solutions.

Significant new function implies multiple overlapping new UIs supporting multiple tasks, which interact with each other in ways that are not yet well understood. It implies multiple roles—4-6 are typical. The team needs to use the full range of research and design tools to understand the practice and design the solution concept. Here is a rough description of how such a project can be structured. Fuller details on each part can be found in *Contextual Design*[20].

Example 6.2 Typical problem statements indicating the need to start with a strategic design phase.

"We need to be the next iPhone in our domain."

"We are purchasing a new enterprise software system and need to tailor it to support our business."

"We need to revamp our product to deal with a changing market."

The team needs to understand the work practice and the design more thoroughly. They will need to start with a robust user research process. The team should start with 15-30 CIs to understand the work practice, looking at the tasks and work context to be addressed by the next version. They build an affinity and sequence work models to represent the issues and the tasks as they are currently done. If whole workgroups or multiple workgroups are to be supported, they will probably want a flow model and may want other work models from Contextual Design as well.

Table 6.1: Supporting a new release with an 8-week phase 0. This structure gathers data from 12 users, supporting 3-4 roles. If your organization will not tolerate spending 8 weeks on phase 0, this can be scoped back by reducing the number of interviews (and, therefore, the number of roles that can be supported) or by eliminating one or both rounds of paper prototype testing. Just remember, if you eliminate these rounds, you can expect to need more iteration with users during the sprints.

	Mon	Tues	Wedns	Thurs	Fri
Wk 1 AM	2 parallel customer interviews	2 parallel customer interviews	2 parallel customer interviews	2 parallel customer interviews	Data cleanup and planning
PM	2 interp sessions	2 interp sessions	2 interp sessions	2 interp sessions	
Wk 2 AM	2 parallel customer interviews	2 parallel customer interviews	Build affinity	Build affinity	Build affinity
PM	2 interp sessions	2 interp sessions			
Wk 3 AM	Consolidate models	Consolidate models	Walk affinity and models	Vision	Vision
PM					
Wk 4 AM	Storyboard	Storyboard	Storyboard	UED	UED
PM					
Wk 5 AM	UI design	UI design	UI design	Build paper prototypes	Build paper prototypes
PM					
Wk 6 AM	2 prototype interviews	2 prototype interviews	Resolve design issues	Redesign	Redesign
PM	Interpret both	Interpret both			
Wk 7 AM	Build paper prototypes	Build paper prototypes	2 prototype interviews	2 prototype interviews	Resolve design issues
PM			Interpret both	Interpret both	
Wk 8 AM	Redesign	Redesign; final cleanup	Write user stories	Write user stories	Release planning
PM					
Wk 9 AM	Start sprint 1				
PM					

They respond to the data with a visioning process, doing multiple visions with the whole project team and key stakeholders as necessary, and capturing their approach with a single consolidated vision. This vision covers, at a high level, the whole of the work practice to be transformed by the solution.

Then, because the work practice is more complex and the interaction between task and system is more involved, the team uses storyboards to work out the interaction between user and system. The storyboards are brought together in a User Environment Design to show the system's structure: how function is organized into coherent screens, with access between them, supporting all the different tasks users may be engaged in.

The high-level system structure captured in the UED is tested by developing rough UIs, prototyping them in paper, and testing them in two rounds of user interviews. In the experience of the authors, two rounds of testing resolves fundamental issues of basic structure and function. (Detailed UI design can be done by individual work streams.)

At this point, the overall solution is designed. The high-level function and structure are known. The solution is coherent and consistent, providing integrated support to the whole of users' work practice. From this high-level solution, individual work streams can be defined. Each of these work streams is its own agile project. Each work stream has limited scope, can be implemented by a team of 5-15 people, and has a well-defined deliverable. Each work stream does the work described in Chapter 5: an abbreviated phase 0 to work out the details of their component, release planning to define their specific stories, and sprints validated and iterated with users. Phase 0 can be abbreviated because the component builds on the data and design from the strategic project, but they are likely to need detailed task information and low-level UI design.

The key point here is that a large, strategic project needs more process support than a simple system change. Agile methods excel at taking a well-defined product of limited scope and producing useful working software quickly. But when the scope is very large, research, design, and planning work needs to precede agile development to create a coherent system.

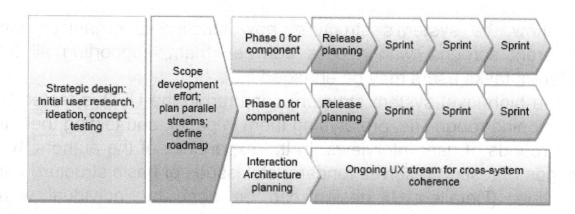

Figure 6.1: The structure of a large-scale agile project. Strategic design and planning sets direction and defines parallel work streams on different components. Each component does detailed design based on user data followed by agile sprints. A UX stream maintains coherence across the entire development effort.

CHAPTER 7

Conclusion

Every ten years or so, a new enthusiasm sweeps through the software development community. Structured Design, Object-Oriented Design, the Rational Unified Process, and now agile Development have all had their day. The fads come and go, but each one leaves behind a valuable residue that becomes part of the permanent toolkit: programmers still structure code according to the principles of structured design, developers still organize function into self-contained objects, and when the agile boom passes, we can expect that software projects will still organize development in short, well-defined sprints each delivering testable user value. The current enthusiasm over agile methods may be a fad, but agile, iterative development is probably here to stay.

Agile development and user-centered design are a natural fit. Agile development assumes an intimate connection to users, and user-centered design assumes rapidly iterating designs with users. To the extent that there is a disconnect between the two, it has more to do with the widely different history and provenance of the two methods rather than any inherent incompatibility.

UX professionals should be—and, we are confident, will be—critical members of any agile team. Where that has not yet happened, what is most needed is an understanding on both sides of the attitudes, values, and skills of the other. Once UX professionals understand the commitment of agile development to the customer and the flexibility of agile development to change, they can open up to the just-in-time, low-overhead style of agile teams. And once developers understand the advantages of user research and prototyping in the field, they will be able to see how doing some of this work up front can make agile development, itself, faster and more problem-free.

Bibliography

[1] Madden W. and Rone K *Design, Development, Integration: Space Shuttle Primary Flight Software System,* CACM 27 9, Sept 1984, 914–925. DOI: 10.1145/358234.358254 3

[2] Boehm B. "A Spiral Model of Software Development and Enhancement," *IEEE Computer.* 21(5), 61–72. DOI: 10.1145/12944.12948 3

[3] Schwaber K. and Beedle M. *Agile Software Development with Scrum.* Prentice Hall, Upper Saddle River, NJ, 2001. 3

[4] Beck K. *eXtreme Programming Explained: Embrace Change,* second edition. Addison-Wesley, 2004. 6, 21

[5] Martin A., Biddle R., and Noble J. "XP Customer Team: A Grounded Theory" in *Proceedings of the Agile 2009 Conference* (Agile 2009), pp. 57–64. IEEE Conference Publishing Services, 2009. DOI: 10.1109/AGILE.2009.70 6

[6] Victor B. and Jacobson N. "We Didn't Quite Get It" in *Proceedings of the Agile 2009 Conference* (Agile 2009), pp. 271–274. IEEE Conference Publishing Services, 2009. DOI: 10.1109/AGILE.2009.22 7

[7] Fuqua A. M. and Hammer J. M. "Embracing Change: An XP Experience Report" in *Fourth International Conference on Extreme Programming and Agile Processes in Software Engineering.* (M. Marchesi and G. Succi, Eds.), Springer-Verlag, Genoa, Italy, 2003. DOI: 10.1007/3-540-44870-5_36 11

[8] Kollmann J., Sharp H., and BlandfordA. "The Importance of Identity and Vision to User Experience Designers on Agile Projects" in *Proceedings of the Agile 2009 Conference* (Agile 2009), pp. 11–18. IEEE Conference Publishing Services, 2009. DOI: 10.1109/AGILE.2009.58 11

[9] Kyng M. "Designing for a Dollar a Day," in *Proceedings of CSCW'88: Conference of Computer-Supported Cooperative Work* (pp. 178–188). Portland OR. New York: Association for Computing Machinery. DOI: 10.1145/62266.62281 14

[10] Chung W. and Drummond B. "Agile @ Yahoo! From the Trenches" in *Proceedings of the Agile 2009 Conference* (Agile 2009), pp. 113–118. IEEE Conference Publishing Services, 2009. DOI: 10.1109/AGILE.2009.41 14

[11] Martin A., Biddle R., and Noble J. "XP Customer Practices: A Grounded Theory" in *Proceedings of the Agile 2009 Conference* (Agile 2009), pp. 33–40. IEEE Conference Publishing Services, 2009. DOI: 10.1109/AGILE.2009.70 17, 19, 23

[12] Goguen J. "Formality and Informality in Requirements Engineering," *Proceedings of the IEEE International Conference on Requirements Engineering,* IEEE CS Press, Los Alamitos, CA 1996. DOI: 10.1109/ICRE.1996.10005 17

[13] Greenbaum J. and Kyng M. *Design at Work: Coöperative Design of Computer Systems.* Hillsdale, N.J.: Lawrence Erlbaum Associates, 1991. 17

[14] Wixon D. and Ramey J. *Field Methods Case Book for Product Design.* John Wiley & Sons, Inc., NY, NY, 1996. 17

[15] Beyer H., Holtzblatt K., and Baker L. "An agile customer-centered method: Rapid Contextual Design" in *Proceedings of the XP/Agile Universe Conference 2004,* pp. 50–59. Springer Berlin/Heidelberg, 2006. DOI: 10.1007/b99820 18

[16] Takats A. and Brewer N. "Improving Communication between Customers and Developers" in *Agile 2005.* (M. L. Manns and W. Wake, Eds.), IEEE Computer Society, Denver, Colorado. DOI: 10.1109/ADC.2005.30 19

[17] Sy D. "Adapting Usability Investigations for Agile User-Centered Design" *in Journal of Usability Studies,* Volume 2, Issue 3, May 2007, pp. 112–132 22

[18] Schwaber K. *Agile Project Management with Scrum.* Microsoft Press, Redmond, WA, 2004, p. 137. 22

[19] Maples C. "Enterprise Agile Transformation: The Two-Year Wall" in *Proceedings of the Agile 2009 Conference* (Agile 2009), pp. 90–95. IEEE Conference Publishing Services, 2009. DOI: 10.1109/AGILE.2009.62 22

[20] Beyer H. and Holtzblatt K. *Contextual Design: Defining Customer-Centered Systems,* Morgan Kaufmann Publishers Inc., San Francisco, (1997). 27, 31, 51

[21] Whiteside J., Bennett J., and Holtzblatt K. "Usability Engineering: Our Experience and Evolution," *Handbook of Human Computer Interaction,* M. Helander (Ed.). New York: North Holland, 1988. 28

[22] Seaton P. and Stewart T. "Evolving Task Oriented Systems" in *Human Factors in Computing Systems CHI '92 Conference Proceedings,* May 1992, Monterey, California. DOI: 10.1145/142750.142900 28

[23] Johnson P. 1988. "Task-related knowledge structures: analysis, modeling and application." In Jones, D.M. & Winder, R. (eds), *People and computers IV : proceedings of the fourth conference of the British Computer Society Human-Computer Interaction Specialist Group,* University of Manchester, 5–9 September 1988. Cambridge; NewYork: Cambridge University Press, cl988. 28

[24] Snyder C. *Paper Prototyping: The Fast and Easy Way to Design and Refine User Interfaces.* 2003, Morgan Kaufmann Publishers, San Francisco, CA 40

Author's Biography

HUGH BEYER

Hugh has more than 25 years of experience building and designing applications, systems, and tools. He is co-founder and CTO of InContext Design, a company bringing user-centered design to development teams since 1992. Hugh was one of the pioneers working with Agile teams to bring a strong user interaction design focus to Agile development efforts, reconciling careful UX design with the fast iterations and minimal up-front planning core to Agile approaches.

Before co-founding InContext, Hugh acted as lead developer and architect in a range of systems at Digital Equipment Corp. His domains of experience include object-oriented repositories, databases, and integrated software development environments. Since starting InContext, Hugh has overseen the design of applications from desktop to web to mobile, and from enterprise to small business to consumers in the wide variety of industries supported by InContext.

He holds a B.S. degree in Applied Mathematics from Harvard.

Printed in the United States
by Baker & Taylor Publisher Services